MOTHERPUPPIN' ADORABLE

WHAT TO DO WHEN YOUR DOG IS BETTER THAN EVERYONE ELSE'S.

QUARTETTE

PUBLISHING

www.thepopularpets.com

ISBN: 978-1-7374146-0-5 (print)
ISBN: 978-1-7374146-1-2 (ebook)

Ordering Information:
Special discounts are available on quantity purchases by corporations, associations, and others. For details, contact www.thepopularpets.com

MOTHERPUPPIN' ADORABLE

WHAT TO DO WHEN YOUR DOG IS BETTER THAN EVERYONE ELSE'S.

KENDRA CLARK

DEDICATION

To all of the Adorables in my life past and present: Betsy, Bobby, Farley, Dave, Meg, Dolly, Daisy, Violet, Mikey, Baker, Alice, Mancha, Anza, Dozer, Zooey, Shelby, Skipper, and so many more for inspiring these pages and celebrating life's milestones with me. You all achieved Adorable status in my heart and certainly deserve it from the universe. Your stories will not go unseen as these pages reflect the learnings of our many, many missteps.

INITIATION:
HELLO WORLD, MEET ADORABLE

A dog was what you wanted. Nothing was more certain.

Maybe he came wrapped in a bow on Christmas Day or maybe you spent months researching the Adorable you wanted to take home and spoil. Or perhaps you found him roaming the streets and you decided to protect him from danger and adopt him.

You realized that the tag with the phone number hanging from his collar was not the puppy's cell phone but belonged to someone who may be looking for him. When they didn't pick up by the third ring, you considered hanging up as you waited with bated breath to determine if he could be a permanent member of your family. No answer! He is yours!

Your pursuit of a dog may have been initiated by a soft gaze or a gentle snuggle of a roommate's puppy, harkening you back to your childhood sidekick. It could have been a surge of love from a friend or roommate's furry companion, or just that you enjoy watching your significant other sweep up fur.

No matter, you have finally accomplished your dream, and a dog has been welcomed into your home with gusto. But what now?

You believe your dog has distinctive, innate qualities that are surely recognizable in Miley Cyrus, Meryl Streep, Serena Williams, and any other icon that recently bombarded the media and caused you to do a double take. Your dog is special, a cut above. She has a certain *Je ne sais quoi*.

Inherent greatness can be revealed when one takes the time to draw it out.

When we use the term "Adorable" in this we book we mean what your darling already is, as well as what she may become.

An Adorable is loved by all, and is irresistible not just to you, but to the public at large. People will scream when they see her as a puppy. They will want to see photos of her every move and outfit.

Now, it's up to you. Time to rise to the occasion! It is your inalienable right and duty to clear the path to fandom for her in true bulldozer fashion so she may obtain true Adorable status.

Taking this path, however, is long, hard, and unclear but necessary if your dog is to be irresistible to everyone you meet in person and virtually.

You did not have to be born into a dog-loving family or grow up with dogs to accommodate their needs. Everyone at any time can usher a dog into their lives and make her irresistible to all.

WHAT THIS BOOK CAN DO FOR YOU AND YOUR ADORABLE

Within this book you will find practical advice about embracing life with a dog and revealing her irresistible nature to the world, from fashion and accessories, dog trivia, social media strategies, party tips, and what car to drive for your pooch to arrive in the custom of a true Adorable. From this day forward all of this and more is arranged so that your Adorable receives optimum love and attention that will pay off the enormous cost of a mammoth collection of dog outfits.

So, stop worrying about your dog's confusion between hardwood table legs and chew toys. Put aside the fact that her breath comes out at a whopping 26,000 BTUs[1] and the odor (which resembles a field of rotten cauliflower) will prevent her from being loved by all.

Your dog will be able to travel through life with effortless grace and confidence, winning over strangers like she was born into the world with drool like silk weave, breath like cinnamon, and farts like roses.

You'll learn that charm and irresistibility win the day, even when you find yourself stranded without a poop bag. You'll never have the dilemma of whether you should bring your dog on vacation or leave her behind as this book has you covered, and as a result, your Adorable is covered too.

Let's be honest: your dog is a star, better than all others, and will be irresistible to all—she is an innate Adorable.

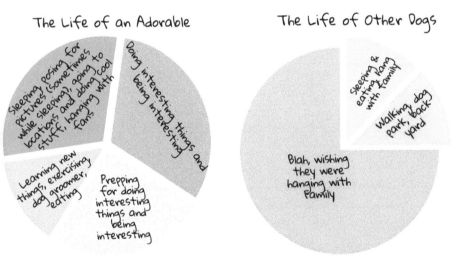

The Life of an Adorable

Sleeping, posing for pictures (sometimes while sleeping), going to cool locations and doing cool stuff, hanging with fans

Doing interesting things and being interesting

Learning new things, exercising, dog groomer, eating)

Prepping for doing interesting things and being interesting

The Life of Other Dogs

Sleeping & eating Rarely with Family

Walking, dog park, back yard

Blah, wishing they were hanging with family

---

1   The **British thermal unit** (BTU or Btu) is a unit of heat; it is defined as the amount of heat required to raise the temperature of one pound of water by one degree Fahrenheit. It is often used by pet lovers to assess the discomfort of standing in close proximity to the output of their pet's breath on a summer day.

TABLE OF CONTENTS

CHAPTER 1

THE PERFECT NAME FOR THE PERFECT ADORABLE

"Esperanza La Mancha!" a woman screamed through the forest, extra loud over the diesel engine of a pick-up truck. Earlier in the day the driver of the truck had adopted Mancha, a small, earless, feisty, and nervous cattle dog mix from a local opera singer, who had found her in a shelter in Mexico. Mancha, upon arriving at her new home, darted into the forest, at which point the opera singer had to be summoned. Mancha had survived having her teeth kicked in, being a bait dog for fighting dogs, two years in a shelter after being found dying in a ditch, and now, finally at her forever home, had run off. Of course, the opera singer agreed to come back and help although it would have to wait until after her opera performance.

The melodic yet bellowing operatic voice echoing through the forest brought neighbors out of their homes with questions and curious looks. But did Mancha even know her name? Perhaps she did, perhaps not, but now the entire town certainly did. Eventually, she returned, and her new roommates peered out the window the next morning to find her joyously ripping apart a blanket in the front yard. For the next 12 years she lived a happy life, but she was never called Esperanza La Mancha again. It did not fit this scrappy little survivor, who had a hard enough time garnering the love and adoration of most, due to her tendency to grab onto a heel now and again, her lack of ears, and her rarely seen toothless grin.

"That which we call a rose
By any other name would smell as sweet."
Juliet, Romeo and Juliet

According to Juliet, Romeo would still be perfect, even if he were not called Romeo. However, even though Juliet bore the pressures of feuding families she did not have the pressures of modern-day society to contend with.

Adorable names matter and set the stage for invoking that "Aww." In the end, what we name our dog mirrors and contains some of our most deeply held hopes and profoundly felt intuitions. Our ultimate selection will serve as a genre guide and point toward our dog being what we most want him to be or connect us to a cherished memory or bucket list aspiration.

Another consideration is name length. Given the prevalence your dog will surely have in your life, his name will get used a lot: called loudly when he may run off, used in conversations with or about your Adorable, used to give direction, and used in your IG handle, posts, and comments to other posts. Imagery is helpful here. Picture yourself calling your dog at a dog park, introducing him to the attractive neighbor on a plane or in the neighborhood, or to a new boyfriend. Like your online dating profile name (later discussed) so much will be revealed with the name of your dog.

CREATING CONNECTION:
NAME CATEGORIES TO FOSTER CONNECTION

Experts suggest that a positive first impression is created by fostering a connection. Do this when selecting a name by harkening back to the familiar in a new way.

1. Liquor or cocktail. The '80s were chock full of beige cocker spaniels named Brandy because brandy, for some reason, topped the liquor bestseller list during that era, which was also known for pop culture that invokes nostalgia for anyone who lived through it. Words like parachute pants certainly trigger in the brain an instant association but rather than MC Hammer, Brandy invokes the association of the warm fuzzies brought on by a sip or two of the beverage itself. Nowadays around and about the dog park it is more common to hear this conversation: "His name is Tito." "Oh, that's my favorite vodka" = connection established. Dog parks also seem to abound with Whiskeys, seemingly mostly for the older set that would actually rather be at home in an easy chair with both whiskeys close by.

2. Note: Certain alcohols, such as ouzo or Jägermeister remove all inhibitions quickly and could bring back memories that have been smartly buried deep into the psyche and locked away forever. So, as cute as it would be to have a dog named Kamikaze, there may not be an equally positive connection developed with your Adorable.

3. Botanicals. Think Sage, Fern, Cedar: unique and in touch with nature.

4. Note: Stay away from poisonous varieties, e.g., hemlock, due to the negative connotation.

5. Flowers: Violet, Daisy, and Rose. But finding an appropriate flower may be tricky for a male Adorable.

6. Note: Stay away from poisonous varieties, e.g., oleander, due to the negative connotation.

7. Official titles. This can be ironic, such as Sergeant Boxcar, Mrs. Dazzle, Inspector X, Surgeon General. Length can be an issue with a title, but titles will instantly evoke a persona that can be cute and satirical.

8. Note: Titles like "The Lovemeister" or the "Bootyshaker" aren't real titles.

9. From the stars. If there was ever a built-in persona, it comes with stealing the name of a well-known icon. The stars have a professional staff that crafted their name, so why not use it too and make it your dog's own? "J.Lo, come!"

10. Note: Stay away from names from stars plagued with improprieties such as instance of petty theft or alcohol and drug abuse , as opposed to a more positive categorical association.

11. Human names. Forget Oreo and go for a human name, the more old-school the better. For an ironic and loving twist, think a riff on Aunt Albertha or Uncle Gaylord.

Amber Zoe
@imamberzoe   • • •

I just found out the dog in the house behind mine is called Brian. I bloody love dogs with proper human names, hahaha!

9:30 PM · 16K   Tweet For You

100K   Retweets   100MK   Likes

12. Hybrids. These can be powerful. After all it took several years for Jennifer Lopez and Ben Affleck to get past "Bennifer." A hybrid could capture you and your significant other's last name or many other unique combinations that will surely lead to a connection and discussion points. It's worth having a Plan B, however, in the event the relationship does not work out as disassembling a hybrid can be worse than covering up a tattoo of "John Forever." Note: You can combine Jennifer, Lopez, or J.Lo with any name and eventually it will be known by all.

13. Cars. Just as celebrities have spent millions on their personas, car companies have spent millions developing the feeling that driving and owning a particular car will evoke. "Bentley, sit!"

You choose your angle but the path to adoration all starts with the name.

NAMES WITH AN INTERNATIONAL FLAIR

You can create a conversational bond by naming your dog from your destination bucket list. Selecting a name of international origin opens up the possibilities driven by a bucket list desire; memories of a trip crossed off the bucket list; or the origin of your dog's breed. Or it can suggest that you are simply fascinated with a culture and ascribe such a persona to your mixed breed. The land of anime, samurai, and sushi provides ample inspo, or get ideas from Tibet and the high Himalayas, or maybe the Isle of Skye, or beyond. Look to Scotland with its rich history and culture, or turn to the romance of the Italian language or the evocative and commanding sound of German. Looking to the international adds a ton of additional options not only for name ideas but for the ultimate personas that will inevitably follow.

NAME	COUNTRY OF ORIGIN
Adele	France
Mignon	France
Conan	Ireland
Finn (also Finnegan)	Ireland
Grady	Ireland
Muriel	Ireland
Hiro	Japan
Taro	Japan
Rufine	Italy
Tito	Italy
Norbu	Tibet
Alisdair	Scotland
Fergie (also Fergus)	Scotland
Barclay	Scotland
Santo	Spain
Britta	Germany
Franz	Germany
Frieda	Germany
Greta	Germany
Zelda	Germany

Not just a singer, this name means "noble," and would suit a mixed breed. Typically, a name that is very appealing to middle-aged men.

You may think steak, but it means "cute" or "dainty," perfect for large dog, like a mastiff or a Great Dane. Unfortunately, there is a high likelihood of confusion with those cute, mumbling Pixar characters, Minions.

Not merely an '80s movie reference, but a legendary name meaning "little wolf" or "gentle giant," this is perfect for a cairn terrier. Expect a few Arnold Schwarzenegger jokes.

Meaning "white" or "fair," suitable for a hearty dog like a Labrador.

A mixed breed could be a match for this name, which means "noble and illustrious."

This harkens back to the movie Muriel's Wedding, but also means "of the bright sea." A pug or bullmastiff would wear it nicely but their charges should be prepared to have a strangely contorted face while speaking it.

Meaning "generous," a characteristic of most dogs. Picture a flouffy mutt with this name. Your dog may be confused with search and rescue dogs who are the real Hiro's.

Meaning "large son." Fitting for any breed.

Meaning "red hair" but suited to breeds other than just an Irish setter.

Reminiscent of an Italian mobster or craft vodka —think Chihuahua, Havanese.

Norbu means "jewel." Any dog could rock this name.

Meaning "leader" but also consider whether this will evoke thoughts of an underwear-less kilt-wearing type. Suitable for a wire-haired pointer or vizsla. Difficult to shorten into a cute nickname which is why most Scottish kids with this name go by Shamus.

If you can stop yourself from thinking of the duchess, then this one is really cute and comes with a male equivalent. Most children given the name Fergus change their name to Alasdair.

Means "birchwood" or, for most, a banking institution fraught with scandal. It's cute and stoic, nonetheless. You can spell it with a "K" ("Barklay") to be extra pawsome.

A "holy" name for a dignified dog. A fine name for a Labrador or other solid companion.

A powerful name for a female dog, meaning "strength" and "exalted one." Best if your dog has thick legs and can bark the word, "Ja."

Meaning "free man," although most of us will immediately think of a muscled bodybuilder who could fall into "'roid rage" at any moment. Suitable for a small breed dog. You must get a second dog named "Hans."

Meaning "peaceful ruler," this name really could suit any dog as most if not all end up ruling a household to a certain extent. This name means that someone should be removed from incarceration.

Meaning "pearl," this name would be fitting for any dog.

Meaning "gray fighting maid," this name is often associated with pit bulls but mostly is just a great name. People say that eventually, anyone or anything named Zelda will end up hurting you.

Dear Kendra,

I was recently lucky enough to rescue a kind and gentle Irish wolfhound. Her name upon arriving was Keres. When I looked up the meaning of the name it appears it means "evil spirits" and that it can be unlucky.

I am prone to bad luck in my life and have been advised by Buddhist monks about karma (they suggested that my bad luck is spiritual retribution; perhaps for past life wrongdoings, or wrongdoings that I committed in this life).

Regardless, my new pup was going to be a new leaf, a new beginning, and now this!

Can I change her name? Will she be confused?

Sincerely,
—Unluckiest

. . . .

Dear Unluckiest,

Step number one is to banish the word "unlucky" and all such labels and descriptions of yourself and replace with more fortunate ones! If not for any other reason than being the proud roommate of a stunning new pup! Irish wolfhounds are incredible and very smart dogs (like all dogs).

Aside from the bad luck omen of this name it is just dumb. How about turning over a new lucky four-leafed beginning and calling her Kendra! This is a great choice for the following reasons, (1) I am lucky—at least I tell myself I am, (2) the similarity in phonics will reduce confusion for her, and (3) I could use a respectable namesake!

Good LUCK,

Kendra

Our Discerning Pet

A story goes that one year after a couple began dating, they moved in together and met with a breeder of Labradors. While waiting on their soon-to-be-born they grew impatient and began perusing the various pet rescue websites and crooned at all the hopeful dogs, viewing their perfect poses and reading their expertly copywritten descriptions. They were overcome by the thought that these endearing faces may not find forever homes.

The deposit they'd left with their breeder, equal to one month's rent, was quickly forgotten as they found an online companion that they knew was meant for them: a gorgeous terrier mix that somehow had not been snatched up and adopted—what luck! They felt a certain connection through their iPad. She seemed to be staring right at them with a gleam in her eye, and they knew she was special. They soon became fully preoccupied with visions of beach walks, coffee dates with her perched nicely at their feet, and lazy Saturday mornings with her jumping on their bed for a morning play. These visions occupied their minds until they were able to get an appointment to visit her. They waited eagerly in anticipation of the surefire blissful relationship with their dog.

When they arrived at the appointment the instant bond was clearly mutual. They made immediate plans to empty their bank account for the adoption fee and supplies they knew she deserved; they'd need a new car, of course—a simple sedan would no longer do—and all future bucket listed travel plans had to be reorganized.

However, when they arrived home their gal began to assert herself in very distinctive ways. She flatly refused her kibble and would only eat home-cooked meals with a drizzle of bone broth and flavored hemp spray; she turned her nose up at her cozy bed and crate and insisted on a fur-lined Pup Protector blanket being placed on the couch or cozily tucked in between the couple in their own bed. They soon observed that they had begun to adjust their seating, often times sitting on the floor to accommodate her needs, and would wake up with crooked necks as she stretched out to form the middle of an H throughout the night.

As they began to take her on various play dates at the park or with friends, they noticed she commanded attention, like a natural-born leader. Their dreams of her at their feet at the local cute coffee shop were not as they had imagined; she insisted on occupying a chair of her own at the table, which was not entirely welcomed by all patrons, who looked on as she daintily lapped her water from a cup without noise or spills.

She also refused any water from any shared bowl and would only drink if the couple used their own Fiji water from their stainless-steel bottle.

The other dogs in the park got excited by fetch with a ball, stick, or really anything available. But she refused any sort of typical play activities, which seemed contrary to her breed characteristics and instead just gravitated toward their new Allbirds.

They started an Instagram account for her as they were taking pictures anyway and it quickly grew to be quadruple the size of their own.

The first few years with their girl have been an adjustment. The couple hope to one day soon get engaged and had always envisioned their pet being a part of their wedding but they now fear that she will object to being relegated to any role other than the star of the show—and that role will be taken. They truly believe that they adopted an Adorable as to call her anything else just does not seem right.

CHAPTER 2

THE ADORABLE INFLUENCER: HOW TO CREATE AN ONLINE PRESENCE FOR YOUR PUP

Social media will be the cornerstone of your dog's path to fame. But it must seem like an accident. Originally intended to update friends and family on a person's whereabouts and activities, social media is now the perfect vehicle for exposing your dog's wonderfulness to the world. Working across multiple platforms can be helpful but can also lead to burnout, which then begs the question: "What is the correct platform for me?" Most answers lead to Instagram, which has worked since its inception to propel Adorables into common household names but like anything, that hypothesis could be off. This handy quiz should settle it.

QUIZ

WHAT SOCIAL MEDIA PLATFORM IS RIGHT FOR MY ADORABLE?

1. What do you envision your Adorable using a social media platform for?

A. Share imagery that will bring out an "Aww," a like, and a follow.

B. Notify his friends and foes about what a cool life he is leading, with a lengthy description of said cool life.

C. Engage in political discourse regarding any newsworthy item but mostly those surrounding the treatment of animals and poor general quality of commercial pet food.

D. Learn about upcoming job openings and connect with recruiters.

E. Participate in lengthy chatroom discussions about various self-improvement tactics.

2. What does your Adorable hope to bring to a social media platform?

A. Share positivity and a beautiful aesthetic, that mostly ends with an "Aww," a like, and a follow.

B. Entertain and show off his creative side with video content without him having to learn how to type.

C. Share his opinion on several topics, including the inferior quality of commercial pet food and the treatment of animals.

D. Inspire discussion on how to build a stronger bond with one's charge and why commercial pet food is so brightly colored, then sharing what he learns with others.

E. Give advice related to various self-improvement tactics.

3. Choose the word that best relates to your Adorable

A. Aww.

B. Ugh.

C. Ruff.

D. Ruff-ruff (please be quiet).

E. Oral discourse (we know, two words).

4 When someone finds your Adorable on social media what do you want them to do?

A. Follow and like and be in constant wonder about whether your Adorable will go to the dog park next or on a hike.
B. Stay tuned for any future opportunities to contemplate his video content.
C. Stay tuned for his interesting perspective on world events.
D. Try to locate your Adorable based on your check-ins for a seemingly impromptu meeting, which may include sitting outside your home with a bagful of hotdogs.
E. Join a room.

5 What is your Adorable's favorite type of content?

A. Follow and like and be in constant wonder about whether your Adorable will go to the dog park next or on a hike.
B. Stay tuned for any future opportunities to contemplate his video content.
C. Stay tuned for his interesting perspective on world events.
D. Try to locate your Adorable based on your check-ins for a seemingly impromptu meeting, which may include sitting outside your home with a bagful of hotdogs.
E. Join a room.

If you answered mostly (a) then your Adorable really does belong on Instagram. Since Instagram is a free, online photo-sharing application and social network platform that has more and more capabilities each day that mirror other platforms, this is a smart move. Photos of your Adorable can be edited and uploaded, along with short videos with a catchy caption that your Adorable will serve as inspo for.

If you selected any answer referencing "video" you may be a closet TikToker or YouTube star but honestly, for now, your Adorable's fan base demographic is on IG so thankfully he can use those video creation skills with the new features of the app.

If you selected mostly (b), (c), or (d) it may be that your Adorable either feels the need to have an inbox full of messages from recruiters, is trying to engage with the granny set, or wants to concentrate more on witty quips (which all point to LinkedIn, Facebook, and Twitter respectively). If that's the case, he likely did not understand the questions and he should retake the quiz until all answers are (a) and then continue with the rest of the book. If he answered (e) he may likely have a puppy pal that invited him to Clubhouse, which although seems like a fun endeavor is completely inappropriate since the pal will never actually see how adorable your Adorable is with this social media app.

Pets and their cuteness are the apple of their parents' eye but if managed right can also be the apple of the entire 500 million users of Instagram's eyes. Even better, dogs fit naturally with the platform as their adorableness throughout the day is perfect fodder for the creative imagery that Instagram demands. Human hands and neurons are twitching involuntarily, waiting for your someone's next post. Why not your little buddy's? Say to yourself now, "Why not [insert puppy name here]?"

Whether strutting their stuff around the apartment, wagging their tails, or eating paper towels, it's obvious your dog has a certain allure and is destined for fame…Instagram fame! After all, "Everyone thinks they have the best dog. And none of them are wrong," said W.R. Purche. (If you don't deeply believe that right now, close the book and throw it out the window.)

However, is cuteness enough? Heck, no! No barking way!

BEFORE YOU GET STARTED

1. Seek inspiration. You need to check out the competition. This is a meme-eat-meme world. If you are a dog fan it's likely you have been following some top accounts already, however, that was for amusement's sake. Now that you desire to join those ranks, revisit those accounts with a fresh eye. For inspiration check out top accounts like @itsdougthepug or @jiffpom or @tunameltsmyheart which are some of the most popular accounts at the time of this writing. In particular, notice the voice they use, dog or person, layout, image selection, and personality. All accounts have a defined personality reflected in the breed characteristics (and in the case of @ tunameltsmyheart a lack of orthodonture characteristic) and two of them communicate from the perspective of the dog, rather than the poster. No strategy is an island, and, as say many in the Marines, who are all dog owners: "The enemy gets a vote."

2. Think about your angle. The most successful accounts typically have an angle that they present consistently. What is your little hero's story?

SEEK INSPIRATION – CHECK
OUT OTHER ACCOUNTS

Note creative inspiration is not the same as copying.

a. Theme. For example, the IG famous @mensweardog. He appears to have his own personal haberdasher, which is the focus and theme of the account. Think of developing your angle or persona as a sort of avatar that will evoke certain characteristics. Your avatar reflects your pet's personality. @mensweardog would not be so engaging or garner so many followers if the attire were not on a dog that is so ironically fit for such a gimmick. Many men do not look as good in seersucker.

b. Your dog+. Another angle may be your pet and a sidekick, like @whippetsunleashed, which features two dogs or @trooperthedane where Trooper is clearly the main feature, but his housemate comes along for greater posting interest. Beware: the sidekick must be from your household because fame will go to the sidekick's head and you risk having a nasty, online breakup. Think every rock band ever only worse.

c. Account aesthetics. An angle or theme can also be the actual look and feel of the account, like @_wand_wand where the angle is stunning photos in monochrome. A brand that rose to success due to their gorgeously curated monochrome-themed aesthetic and where no one thought to themselves, "What are they hiding with this chromatic singularity?" A specific, preset filter, from the plethora being pushed on various apps with names like "Holi-day," "Selfie," or "Dog Wonder," can also be an account aesthetic if used consistently. Check out @appa.s_adventures, which features Appa, an Australian Shepherd in Hawaii; his account shows a mix of profiles but all posts are tied together with the same filter and usually a colored bandana, which makes the aesthetic. Appa could be doing very little but the visuals override any lackluster activities.

Bottom line: your angle is critical, and the options are vast but should always be driven by your pet's personality. Aesthetics like color tone or filter or a common item that appears in each post are a great start. See Chapter 3 for more photography tips.

In the end, people need something special to make them remember your dog, and as Sean Griffis, father of the @bonjourbrie points out, you've got to be able to really get into the character and have fun with it without it becoming burdensome for you and your followers to stay consistently invested. Remember, most people have a sexual thought every 11 minutes and want to see a cute puppy shot every 10 minutes. One of the many reasons for a slowing in population growth in "high-dog-owner" countries.

Even though you are driven by an aesthetic theme do not sacrifice authenticity for it; make every photo feel as natural as possible. To really resonate with followers, you must showcase as many real moments of your dog's daily life as possible.

Like any other account, followers should feel like they are getting a peek inside your dog's unique and fabulous existence. If they have fallen in love with them as they should, they'll be waiting impatiently for the next image of your baby taking a nap, wearing a clown nose, and maybe a tuxedo.

As Griffis emphasizes, the more personality you showcase, through both visuals and copy, the more people will connect with your dog. Whatever your dog's day-to-day life involves, try to snap a photo of the number one most engaging moment as many times as possible.

Dear Kendra,

I have been yearning for years to round out my biker aesthetic and MC lifestyle with a tough-looking dog. I was fortunate to find a bullmastiff that I aptly named Tough. I set up my account as @MCbikerandtough and carefully crafted my bio, sure to capture all synonyms related to being tough and avoiding all emojis that infer a jovial attitude. Tough, however, just does not seem into it.

Ultimately, she prefers to settle on my lap in a heated massage chair or have a lick of an ice cream. She is bothered by spiked collars and black leather. She also seems to have an allergy to motorcycle exhaust fumes. I feel like my dream will never come to fruition.

What should I do?
—@MCbikerandtough

....

Dear @MCbikerandtough,

You are correct, your dream is dead. If Tough is not into it, she is not into it and her desires rule when it comes to creating an authentic social media account. You could dress her up in her biker gear and take shots of her doing what she has no affinity for but that would only create stress for you and your girl and would fall flat with your community (if you could even get one, being a faker).

Good news! IG handles and bios can be changed. So, before you embark on an inauthentic journey dig deep and consider if @ toughnotsotough would be a better approach whilst choosing imagery and captions that highlight the sensitive side of your girl. Let us know if you need assistance with the copy of your Craigslist ad for your bike.

Good luck,

3. Kendra **Pick** a strong username or "handle," as referred to in the CB Radio

PERSONAS

Your dog will portray a certain personality which will flow from your photos and captions. Personality and attitudes are authentic and likey line out with the breed and actual dog personality. Most common personalities include:

Joie De Vivre. Excited by life, likely pictures include an open mouth which can be perceived as a smile, a toy, and excitement.

Cynical. Typically a caption discussing boredom, the miserable state of the world, and newsworthy items.

Worldliness. For the traveler or those that like to appear as such, may be dressed up, with a book, frequently in a new locale.

Sophistication. The discerning dog imagery will likely be them sitting at a table or enjoying human delicacies and entertainment.

days. "Give a dog a bad name and hang him," went the old English proverb. There is also a Scottish proverb, "Can I have your dog before you hang him, English?" Nevertheless, "Toe Jam," a popular CB Radio handle just won't do and that's okay because there are a ton of clever, creative usernames to go along with your chosen theme. However, if your dog's name is a common one, e.g., "Max" the good usernames will be taken, so get creative and try not to compromise with underscores or periods in your IG username, which just causes confusion: is the period before the word dog or after?

4. Some people even select their pet's name just to have a great IG

NOTE

Do not limit you and your Adorable's future to our identified personas, thousands of additional ones exist including, but not limited to, Olympic Athlete, Gangster, Medium (All-Knowing), and Beauty Influencer + thousands more!

@tootough

♥ ○ ▽   🔖
MC Sinners Rule Baby
#mcforever

@ninjadog

♥ ○ ▽   🔖
The first rule of being a ninja is, "Do no harm."
#ninjarule

@babyb

♥ ○ ▽   🔖
Having a great hair day but had trouble with the help. I need a slushie!
#firstworldproblems

@dogsliv4fun

♥ ○ ▽   🔖
Another Superfun Day!
#carsaresuperfun

Tough. The dog that is adorned with spikes and leather. Would own a Harley, likely has an owner that does, and is the face of the local motorcycle gang.

Fighter: A Ninja-type theme where the puppy's real identity is never known allowing for usage over many generations.

Bitch. Besides the obvious dog terminology, this Theme is female-centric personna takes-no-prisoner, in-charge... you guessed it... bitch.

Homespun. These are the 'aw shucks' type that enjoys downtime and home fun with unabashed pleasure. You will not find posts of these guys with cucumber slices on their eyes but more often than not, catching a frisbee and hanging from the car window.

handle, like Sean Griffis, with @bonjourbrie. As Sean tells it, as he waited for his puppy to be ready to take home, he mulled over the perfect name for her. Then he landed on @bonjourbrie—partly because he thought it a perfect alliterative Instagram handle and not a typical dog name, and partly as it played into people's love of food and French culture. And, voilà, Brie (@bonjourbrie) was created. Shortly thereafter, @bonjourcheddar turned up, though to little fanfare, whereas a more ingenious thinker chose @adiosenchilada and has a huge following.

5. Create a strong Instagram bio. Adorableness, and therefore the rea-

son to follow your dog, is all about his personality and this should carry through to his bio. It should mention key searchable words, such as Cocker Spaniel, Super Dog Tricks, Traveling Dog, or Van Life, for example (if these are indeed true and reflected in your feed) so people can find you, as well as your dog's breed. If your dog is a whippet and you want to appeal to whippet owners or lovers of monochrome or Hawaii, make sure it's in your bio. Switching to an Instagram business account is free and comes with added benefits and no commitment to actually be profitable or attempt to be profitable (thank goodness).

A business account provides additional space for contact information and allows you to take a deeper dive into your analytics, such as who is liking your posts and when, plus you get some extra real estate for your bio, which you should maximize. Personal info can allow for a good connection, just ensure you are not alienating any potential fans at the same time. Adding "Dedicated Army Fan" to your bio may alienate some potential Navy aficionados, and why do that?

EVERY ADORABLE DESERVES STAR TREATMENT. GET EXCLUSIVE CONTENT AT THEPOPULARPETS.COM

INSTAGRAM BIOS

1. Username. Cute, Adorable, and meaningful. See further guidance above

2. Profile picture. Cute, adorable, and reflective of your Adorable's personality.

3. Use the space where your name should be to tell people a bit about yourself "award winning…" This is also a searchable area!

4. Focus on the first two lines of bio to get the personality across. This will take imagination and creativity on your Adorable;s behalf!

5. You can link out to one website from here. If your Adorable has a website put it here! If he does not—why not??

6. Ensure that people can contact you with Influencer and other opportunities

7. These are called thumbnails and should be a matching icon relating to your Adorable, celebrity friends, and favorite toys

12 BIO IDEAS FOR INSPO

- A taste of my good life. This isn't the full picture—the real thing's far better.

- The toughest thing I've ever tried is to not pee on your lawn.

- Dog years are long…so I smile a lot.

- I like to have my puns created in the most pawsitive way.

- Life is too short to wear ugly collars.

- Single and ready to play chase with someone that I find attractive.

- My relationship status? Frisbees, the couch, and dog treats.

- I enjoy everything like the way people enjoy milk on billboards.

- I don't understand Instagram yet, or have thumbs, yet here I am.

- I eat some steak when I am upset.

- Height is 9", but my personality is 6'1".

- On a quest to remove every squeaker from all dog toys.

To Post or Not to Post

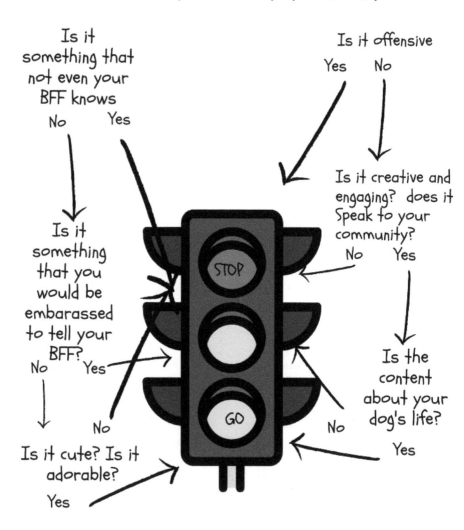

Is it
something that
not even your
BFF knows

No   Yes

Is it offensive

Yes   No

Is it
something
that you
would be
embarassed
to tell your
BFF?

No   Yes

Is it creative and
engaging? does it
speak to your
community?

No   Yes

Is the
content
about your
dog's life?

No

Yes

Is it cute? Is it
adorable?

Yes

No

No

STOP

GO

*Note these are not hard and fast rules.
Ultimately if anything gives you pause you
may want to find another idea.

6.   Curate your content. It has to be good. We know it: Instagram is a
     visual platform so quality, engaging content wins the day. A poorly
     lit, yellow-hued photo of your dog greeting his friend or a feed full
     of your dog sleeping is not reflective of the awesomeness of your
     Adorable. Good content will reflect your amazing dog and anything
     that isn't truly great content will not support your growth or show
     appreciation for your audience. If you couldn't take your images
     and put them in a flip book where they turn into an interesting
     mini-movie you may not be choosing the right images.

Reveal your dog's adorableness by pushing the limits on ingenuity and creativity. Consider timely and trending events (holidays are an easy start—
See Chapter 14) to insert your pet into social media conversations in lieu
of the frontal shot, again! Move from the couch or dog bed, switch up
the location, and take them out into different elements; play with camera
perspectives by shooting them at different angles, and experiment with
product placement. This will show brands that you can be of use down the
road. In the end your dog will "pop" and call out to the vast number of dog
lovers cruising for their next account to love and follow.

Actual posts. Putting it out there. Suggestions vary but most accounts
can grow with three to four posts per week and five stories. Posting really
depends on you. To keep your sanity don't let a posting schedule take over
your life. Not only will the stress of a schedule cause you to lose authenticity, but ultimately you are dealing with a dog, no matter how intelligent and
adorable, who is oblivious to the pressures of social media fame. You can
do it all at once on the weekend right after a nap; put on different outfits
and chase them around the house. Every time they rest take a photo and
change outfits. Ninja dogs can just change bandanas (or bananas). Once
you get great content use scheduling tools like Later so that you can batch
content. Remember, this is supposed to be fun.

Engagement. Be social! Your dog will become famous if he likes, shares,
and contributes. Show appreciation for new followers and love their great
content as well.

Three Steps to Writing as Your Adorable

(also known as Barklingualism)

1 Decide on level of anthropomorphism.* Do you want your Adorable to be a realistic dog, or do you want to give him human emotions, motivations, language, and behavior?

2 Determine what your Adorable is really thinking and feeling and how it is represented by his behavior. (Critical for realistic anthropomorphism*: A dog's reality is different due to size and senses.

3 Determine social structure. Is he the leader of the household (as most Adorables are)? Is she the ringleader at the dog park and amongst their pack or outside of the pack?

*Anthropomorhism: the attribution of human characteristics or behavior to a god, animal, or object

A note on liking, sharing, and contributing. Despite the brain fog when it comes to dogs—also known as judgment being blinded by love—the charge of an Adorable and the Adorables community knows that typing with any sort of efficiency is not done by the Adorable. So, as you take on this great responsibility of liking, commenting, and sharing on behalf of your Adorable you must either do so in their voice or in your own voice, from your perspective. For example, you need to decide if in response to another community member getting a treat you post: "That treat looks so good—I would even roll over for that one," as opposed to, "Those treats look healthy—I feed those to my Adorable as well."

If you are speaking on behalf of your pet, from your perspective, use the Lexicon in Chapter 21 and if your Adorable is having a grumpy day you can leave any inference to a bad mood out of it.

Top tip: Remember the star of the show. Reward your dog for his cooperation and tolerance on his way to fame with treats, toys, walks, and fun if you feel like it.

QUIZ

HAIL, THE INSTAFAMOUS MATCH
THE DOG PERSONA WITH THE ACCOUNT

Emulating is the closest form of flattery, or something like that. You should be familiar with these cute accounts to get inspo but also to understand what makes them special.

@jiffpom	I am a serious outdoorsman.
@itsdougthepug	I have more pastel outfits than you will ever have.
@tunameltsmyheart	I have hung out with Demi Lovato, Shakira, Casey Neistat, Katy Perry, and more. Celebrities love me!
@loki	I am from Michigan.
@tuckerbudzyn	My family believes more is better.
@harlowandsage	I could use braces.

PHOTO INSPO

Every Day Life in the Feed

Everyday life provides rich sources of content possibilities. These are the most basic spots they may be identified as "scenic points" but many more possibilities exist.

If you think that your town is not as vibrant you may be correct, but you can always substitute puddles for ponds along with many more practical substitutions.

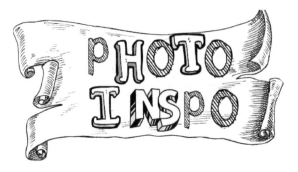

PHOTO INSPIRATION SPOTS IN EVERYDAY LIFE

Content diversity is key: your local town or cityscape provides a rich source of places where you and your pet can build new content and attract new fans!

1. Hills. Face west for a great view of the sunset; good for well-lit shots sitting, standing, or rolling in the grass. Make sure that the sun is behind you, but your shadow in an image will scream rookie.

2. Ponds. Ideal for those swimming and retrieving shots. Reveals athletic abilities and obedience.

3. Tall hedges. Great backdrop, especially for light-colored dogs. The dog will stand out with a color punch against the greenery. Consider matching the bandana to hedges, blooms, or a particular shade of green.

4. Farmers' market. For those where your dog's presence is not a health code violation the fresh fruits and vegetables make a colorful backdrop for photos. Added bonus: great shots with fans among vendors and attendees alike.

5. Kids' park. Kids are sure-fire adoring fans. A meet-up with kids is perfect posting fodder as a shot of your pet going down a slide and playing a quick game of hide and seek will always be a winner and reveal the loving kindness of your pet for all.

6. Library. Great potential shots of returning books for those intellec-

tual pet pals (although never with a book in mouth!). Titles can be shown that reflect a pet's personality and of course using community resources like the library is very sensible and grounding.

7 Play fields. Perfect for all those action shots, if your dog is so inclined: soccer, frisbee, solo-action catches, or with friends he meets that become new besties.

8 Local bar. A patio shot of your Adorable enjoying a refreshment is never overdone. If the establishment allows dogs, they will no doubt appreciate the tag and great post and will welcome you like a local next time you stop in for a refresh.

9 Skate park. The über talented may even get on for a ride. This will take practice that should be done at home in the kitchen but once a short distance is mastered a quick action shot will be a winner.

10 Sidewalk. Leashed or unleashed depending on how strict the ordinance enforcement is and the obedience of your dog. Taking a walk is always good for meeting new and old friends that immediately stop to express how adorable your dog is and ask for a quick pet and inquire about breed origins. A stop on a bench for a shot with friends in front of a cute store is always postable content.

11 Town square. Some towns like Jackson Wyoming and Monterey, California have nice grassy areas for an impromptu picnic. There may be a monument in the town square for a photo backdrop but lounging on the picnic blanket is also a sure-fire adorable shot.

12 Baseball field. Running the bases and crossing the home plate is a testament to your talents as a dog-lover.

13 Fast-moving creeks. The doggy paddle is still the most efficient stroke in everyday use. Being able to cross and swim near ducks that he chased from the pond is an attention-grabber. Swimming across with a license plate or McDonald's cup in mouth shows that your puppy is also clearly "green."

CHAPTER 3

THE ADORABLE CELEBRITY: A GUIDE TO ALL THINGS MEDIA

Preserving memories and gaining adoring fans in everyday life takes a lot of the same effort as reaching celebrity status. But don't get this confused with scrapbooking. If you are on a quest to reach celebrity status you need to be prepared to invest some time and commitment. It won't happen overnight, but there are a few ways to make it more likely your efforts will pay off: good photography, a good portfolio, and a great résumé. Success, where you can use even better adjectives, "stellar," "awesome," and "excellent," is bound to follow.

PHOTOGRAPHY

Photography is the cornerstone for gaining adoring fans. Aspiring models know a high quality, rock solid portfolio is their chance to make a great first impression on agencies and clients alike. The same goes for your pooch as you preserve memories, and adorn walls, social media, and gift cards. You need to put the best paw forward and good photography is your tool. Your dog's next adoring fan is anywhere your pet or your photography is. They may be a top talent scout or Mary from Ohio; it's also possible that Mary from Ohio is two degrees of separation from a top talent scout.

However, getting that star role in the latest *Town and Country* magazine's "Glamour Dog" feature pales in comparison to looking so cute that you get a forever home. Photographers of pet adoptees have the most pressure to gain fans for the pets in their care. The team at Best Friends Animal Society, the largest no-kill sanctuary in the United States, take a serious number of pictures showcasing the pets in their care that are available for adoption. How cute they reveal a pet to be in their photos may be the difference between one of their foster tenants finding a forever loving home or not, and the foreboding "not" is a real issue as it could mean those sad eyes will be continue in life without their sought after plus one. As dedicated dog angels, the pressure is on for them to take some great pics and they, and some others, were kind enough to share some of their secrets:

1. Capture the right light. Indoor lighting near a window provides the best light, but you'll need a reflector to bounce a small amount of light onto the back side of any long facial feature, which could turn off certain adopters. However, outdoors, in the shade or overcast weather is the best. It's important to avoid direct sunlight, especially with a dark-colored dog.

2. If your dog's particular talents demand that you shoot in direct sunlight try to schedule your shoot in the morning or evening when the light is softer. For videos, shoot indoors to control the environment because sound distractions can blow multiple takes and the subject may not be able to come up with the perfect "adopt me" expression more than a handful of times.

3. Capture the eyes. Eye contact with the camera is important for any animal photography but especially for darker animals as the eyes

provide color contrast. To get eye contact make a sharp sound by shaking something or making a sharp noise just above the camera so the dog will turn their head and prick their ears. Try not to make a startling sound that can cause them to feel as if they're being scolded or just plain make them run away at top dog speed.

4. Focus on the right area. Make sure that the feature you want to highlight is in focus, which may mean redirecting the camera's focus. For instance, dogs' long noses cause many with auto focus on their cameras to inadvertently concentrate on the nose instead of on the dog's eyes, so the most attractive feature and insight into their personality ends up blurry. If the dog has multi-colored eyes or eyes that don't match, you can touch those up with Photoshop. A dog with those eyes in the flesh is fine, but in a photograph, they are a deal-breaker. It's the same with crossed eyes, whereas large, protruding bug-eye photos are a big payday and adoption is instantaneous.

5. Go for unique shots. You want to go for shots with personality like an inquisitive look or a goofy pose. There is a motto in dog photography: get those ears up, nose down, and eyes up. There is no acronym for that. The same motto applies for IG stars or for a dog model portfolio. Play up the unique and diverse—there is no standard bikini or fashion shot here; the most popular dogs know they need to get creative and not look like everyone else. A touch of personality goes a long way.

6. Level up or down. Get those glutes working and crouch down to your dog's level. This viewpoint will add a different perspective to your shot. Clearly, Great Dane owners have the upper hand on this one but a new perspective on a level with your dog will offer variety and intimacy with them. Let's be honest: you cannot raise the dog's level and make it look natural. You must go down to the puppy.

7. Action shots. Everyone is taken with a serene, sleeping baby or dog, where peacefulness and innocence abound, but you kind of need

to be physically there in the moment. The ho hum dog bed shot, however, is not engaging or fully revealing of your pet's adorableness. Further, since dog beds are usually dark in color and dogs sleep in poor photography light, the cuteness rarely transitions into your shot. It is easier to show how interesting your pet is with active shots in interesting places. In the end avoid any shot that would remind someone of their senior photo in high school. Dealbreaker.

Dear Kendra,

I am the mother of four boys. We never had the girl I dreamed of and with that went my romanticized vision of trading outfits and makeup tips with a loving daughter. However, my husband found a lovely little female basset hound that has become my faithful sidekick. I named her Lolly and you can find her at @lollybabygirl. Although I have accepted that we won't be sharing make-up tips I have found a tailor to make custom-made outfits for her. However, she does not appreciate my attempts at pet personification and chews them off immediately. I was hoping that she could be the female version of @jiffpom and satisfy my yearnings for a daughter at once but alas it seems that is not to be the case.

—Mother of Five

@lollybabygirl [FOLLOW] ...

143 likes

Hair and makeup day!

Dear Mother of Five,

First, I am sorry about the four boys thing; I have two, and the thought of four is quite shocking. Although I love them to death, the fart jokes from four would be too smelly. Second, you have one of the cutest dogs born! Those with deliciously cute dogs do not need their pet's costume to compete with their dog's cuteness factor or contribute to the pet personification you yearn for. Your pet is adorable enough and a good enough companion without adding a costume and sealing her humiliation as per a teenage boy at his first dance.

Ditch the frilly dresses and try these creative ways to add interest without the typical paired humiliation.

i. Shoot photos in front of a background. Backgrounds can be cute fabrics or a solid wall or mural, in this case a deeply feminine one.

ii. Write a message that is funny or interesting (not for a portfolio but other uses). A chalkboard or other message board with a cute saying is sure to get a read and a chuckle. An appropriate one for you may be, " My brothers have the best sister in the world."

iii. Deploy tasteful props. Hats, bow ties, bandanas, or boas—think of the photo booth props at the last party you attended. Also, absurdist props, such as a fishing pole in the mouth or an accounting book are scroll-stoppers as they instantly raise curiosity, and the viewer may want to know more. Perhaps they'll think they can win the fishing pole or get some good accounting tips.

Either way, let the tailor know that you won't be needing any more custom-made dresses and use the extra savings to buy dog treats for your stellar companion and make a female connection to add some femininity into your life. With the adorableness of a basset you likely need little else but the suggestions above to create an engaging fun feed.

—Kendra

THE LIMITATIONS OF ARTISTIC IMPRESSION.
THE DOS AND DON'TS TO GET THAT ULTIMATE SHOT

Any successful portfolio or IG feed will need to contain an assortment of images—no standard fashion shots allowed. Stopping the scroll and getting a Like or catching the attention of the empowered talent scout requires ingenuity. However, we've all heard about those on the IG Like and Follower quest that have taken things a bit too far, sometimes with disastrous consequences. Going the extra mile is hailed in these parts but here are some things to avoid to ensure your efforts are not for naught.

1. Enjoyment. You might love the parachuting shots and video clips, but your pet may not. Make sure that when you are thrill-seeking your pet is willingly at your side partaking in the joyous activity just as they would be for a quick cuddle. A quivering unhappy guy is not good for the fan base or your pal.

2. Danger. Your dog knows his commands and the seascape is a great background but leaving him on a rock where a rogue wave could carry him off is simply not worth it.

3. Dressing up. Certain dogs pull of the dress-up game well, but others can take serious offense and it will show. The glasses and chef hat may be to die for but don't forget your pet's ego and personality.

4. Authenticity. We hear about being authentic all the time but what does it really mean? A French bulldog in a beret may be as cute as a Chihuahua longingly gazing at a taco while a mastiff would rather have a chew on either and the adorableness would be completely lost. On your quest for that unique shot don't forget to be authentic. Much like the oft quoted threshold test for obscenity: "You'll know it when you see it."

This test may not be that helpful since as later said by William Goldberg, "I know it when I see it," can still be paraphrased and unpacked as: "I know it when I see it, and someone else will know it when they see it, but what they see and what they know may or may not be what I see and what I know, and that's okay." If you are trying too hard to unpack that, you likely neither knew or saw.

@thepopularpets   ...

He knows the password
(Hint: It's his name!) Get exclusive
content with Harry at
thepopularpets.com

QUIZ

DO YOU NEED AN ACTING OR MODELING PORTFOLIO?

Not all photography is to adorn your home and social media. If you are as certain that your dog has what it takes to be the next Toto or spokesperson for PetSmart as you are that next Thanksgiving will be wrecked by your drunken uncle, you need to take this short quiz to see if you have the requisite stage parent abilities and your pet has what it takes to be on the cover or the star of the production. Just ask the most famous stage parent of all time, Mrs. Lohan*. Stage parenting is not for the faint of heart. However, a top score may mean that you need to get that photography portfolio and résumé together ASAP.

1 Being a star requires certain decorum, manners, and basic training. Does your dog have the greatest tendency to

A. Drop on his back with paws in the air when you give him a command.

B. Sniff the crotches of all he meets.

C. Run and grab anything that looks even close to a ball.

D. Follow direction the majority of the time and know how to sit, stay, and lie down when bribed with a treat.

2 You know your dog is adorable, but do others quickly see his beauty? Being on the cover or the star of the show requires your dog to spark an immediate "Aww" from audiences. When you are out and about do people tend to:

A. Share their grooming tips and recommend their own talented groomer, and then say, "Aww."

B. Comment that your dog must have been from an unplanned litter but that he is so fortunate to have found you, and then exclaim, "Aww."

C. Express adoration for your dog's adorableness and ask what breed he is so they can start a Pinterest board, and then shout, "Aww."

3 Your dog cannot drive himself to shoots and casting calls. Being a stage parent is demanding on resources and time. Showing up when needed is critical. The best description of your current time demands is:

A. Leaving work may mean that a life-saving surgery is not done.

B. You have three children that are child actors and constantly on casting calls.

C. You've recently lost your job with no new one in sight, your phone is always close at hand, and you drive an electric vehicle that you can plug in at your neighbor's.

4 There is a reason why child actors typically make headlines outside of their roles. Few of the famous are reclusive. Being on the cover or in a leading role takes an innate willingness to put it out there but, naturally, with a measured eagerness that does not become overwhelming. You would best describe your dog's personality as:

A. Shy and timid; he hides under the table when guests come over.

B. Aggressive and overly protective: neighbors have reported your dog for looking menacingly at them through the fence and you have not been able to employ a house sitter or dog walker due to these proclivities.

C. Independent and outgoing: if your furry friend were a person you suspect he would be doing routines on the bar or stealing the evening with a well-practiced karaoke skit; he often does both with you at more pet-friendly establishments.

D. Shifty; your dog brings home a lot of needles that he acts like he "found."

5 Often, the glamour overshadows the work and dedication it took the famous to arrive at their celebrity status. Stage parents are dedicated to the development of those that have the prospects to be famous and the same fortitude will be required of you and your dog to make it onto the big screen. The best description of you and your dog's daily schedule is:

A. Lying in until noon and then taking in a late brunch on the patio of a local dog-friendly establishment.

B. Hanging out with the local kids at the skate park and marveling at their ambition.

C. Having recently purchased *2,022 Tricks You Can Teach Your Dog*, you are working on number 1,801, all of which are evidenced with well-edited video footage .

6 Social media may be the key to discovery and at the very least will legitimize your fan base for agents and scouts. A quality account with followers is important for the journey to fame. A noun to describe your interaction with social media is:

A. Voyeur: you participate only by leering at others posts and have profiles but no posts and do not comment, like, or share other posts.

B. Rebel: you only post the stupidest content as a form of provocation.

C. Exhibitionist: you believe that life is not for living but for posting. The quest for content drives you and your dog's daily activities.

RESULTS ON THE NEXT PAGE! ⟶

There are no right answers here, however, if you chose (c) or (d) to all of the questions above then you had better start capturing your dog's adorableness and assembling a portfolio ASAP. If you answered (c) more than 50 percent of the time then you may want to get organized, depending on what your other answers were, but some consideration may be in order before you take on this arduous task. If you answered (c) less than 50 percent of the time, you should really take the quiz again and this time think about the questions. Either way, your dog's adorableness will likely be revealed to the world through alternative means than a movie feature or a magazine cover, but you can always revisit when things change for you both. There is a market for senior dogs in roles and photography if this takes longer than expected.

*Mrs. Lohan the most famous stage parent of all time, mother to Lindsey Lohan. Voted by E! Online** readers as the worst parent of the year, not due to her dedication as a stage parent but for her actual parenting skills, which appear to be mutually exclusive.

**E! is for people wh0 actually have the time to care about the Kardashians and tend to eat, sleep, and breathe pop culture. In short, they are informed voters.

GETTING IN

You have decided your dog needs to be on the cover of *Vanity Fair* or the star of the next big sitcom—if only because it would be a shame, with all his attributes, to not. Now you've got to persuade an agent to take you on or a booking agent to schedule an audition. The easiest route to you and your dog's own personalized director's chair is with a quality résumé and photo portfolio. It will not matter that your last attempt at dog stardom resulted in a lifted leg on the casting director's purse. They may overlook that with the right assets this time.

If, after combing your contacts and everyone you have ever given a like to on social media, you find you don't have a personal connection who works the front desk of an agency or temps at the studio, you will have to resort to other means: a stellar résumé and a portfolio distributed to the correct parties. If, despite our tips above, your shots are still on the amateur side, even with the latest iPhone, it may be time to engage the professionals.

When agents see your dedication and investment, they will be far more likely to take a gander, which will inevitably lead to good things.

The résumé, for people and dogs alike, is frequently a stumbling block but in this context we will focus on the dog. You may think that YOU, the stage parent, are the only communicator of your dog's worthiness but there will be times when your dog's résumé will have to do the talking for you.

This is not the same dog résumé filled with past residences and evidence of good behavior used to convince your landlady your Adorable is worthy to live in her walk-up; this résumé must reveal of all your Adorable's talents in one place. It must reflect experience and disciplined vibrancy, letting others know your dog is worth their investment of time and energy.

You need to portray that your Adorable, and by association you, will be famous and that they deserve the accolades for having the foresight to uncover this unique and natural-born star. To do this you must weigh the importance of providing accurate details against certain "facts" that prove your dog's innate stardom.

It's important that you give the illusion of success. A lengthy rendition of awards and features is a must. The feature in *People Magazine* as the cutest dog of 2020 or winner of The Palm Dog Award[2] will be far more impactful than "Leader of the Pack" of your local pet rescue. Who's not going to hire that?

---

2   The Palm Dog Award is an annual alternative award presented by international film critics during the Cannes Film Festival. It is given to the best performance by a canine (live or animated) or group of canines during the festival and is sought after by any Adorable in need of a résumé accolade.

Here is a sample résumé to provide you with inspo.

MAMA JUNE SHANNON
902.100.8888
BETTS, BRUSSELS GRIFFON
8" • SOFT BEIGE COAT • 7 LBS

COMMERCIAL PRINT

"Best Spa Treatments to Enjoy with Your Dog"
Town and Country magazine • *September 2019*

"Is Your Dog an Emotional Support Dog?"
Cosmopolitan magazine • *October 2021*

TELEVISION/FILM

The OC • *August 2020*

AWARDS

Most Adorable
Monta Vista High School, Cupertino, California, 2016

Most Likely to Succeed
Monta Vista High School, Cupertino, California, 2016

TRAINING/BEHAVIORS

The Pout, the Whine, the Beg, daintily laps from tableware, kisses on command

Looks on command include:
I'm so sexy; Who farted?; Is that a UFO?; This isn't my frisbee; Out of jail for 24 hours; and the Sylvester-Stallone-is-shorter-than-I-thought look.

UNIQUE SKILLS[3]

Looks amazing in handbag; walks softly on leather to avoid scratching; does not shed—will not leave hair on cashmere; stellar vehicle and air traveler; not afraid of amusement rides; does not need a leash; is willing to be painted, cries on command, can speak with a British accent.

---

3   These need to be repeatable skills and behaviors.

CHAPTER 4

PUP PRESTIGE: CREATING YOUR ADORABLE'S BRAND

Your Adorable already has a personal brand whether you know it or not. If it is not actively managed, however, it could end up working against him. You need him to stand out from the other pretenders.

A brand is made up of perceptions and because of that you cannot dictate your Adorable's personal brand; you can only influence it and, most importantly, accentuate it. In short, your Adorable's personal brand is a reflection on how he presents himself to the world and is made up of the thousands of small things he does in a day, which become what he is known for. For instance, "Hey, isn't that Harry from down the block that always sniffs my crotch?" Okay, that's a bad example, but you do want more for your Adorable than to be remembered for a few small transgressions.

When thinking about Harry's brand, consider what impression he gives people, and whether or not they desire to be around him; look at what

PERSONAL BRAND IN ACTION

DEVELOPED PERSONAL BRAND

"Marty"
"That dog is awesome. He seems to be so happy and he can fetch a beer and do other crazy tricks. He also knows how to surf!" he said with with immediate recognition.

PERSONAL BRAND REQUIRES MANAGING

"Karen"
"I know that dog. All dogs are awesome. But after meeting her I would never want a Poodle. She does not seem nice." he said with immediate recognition.

UNDEVELOPED PERSONAL BRAND

"Rover"
"I don't think I know Rover. Is he that furry dog?" she said with a quizzical look on her face.

comments they post about him and most importantly how he makes someone feel when they come in contact with him. Then consider how "team" Adorable wants people to think of him, which will be his personal brand. In short, it's time to make a brand plan, think it through, and stick to it.

HARRY'S BRAND PLAN

WHO IS HARRY?

How do people feel when they come in contact with Harry?_____

What are his passions? _____

What does he stand for? _____

What are his strengths? _____

Who is his tribe? _____

Who does Harry want to attract? _____

Who are they: age, gender, species? _____

Where do they live? _____

What are their beliefs? _____

What social media do they use? _____

What is his target audience? _____

Does his target have disposable income? _____

Can he bark the name of his target audience? _____

What fears can you stoke in his target audience that only
Harry can solve? _____

What % of his audience has addictive personalities and can you tap into that
behavior? _____

Does Harry have an enemy? Can you create one? _____

How much edginess can Harry pull off regularly? Can he give the finger? ___

How much cuteness or sweetness can he pull off? (Can he blink
sweetly on command)? _____

What's Harry's back story? _____

Is there a dark past? (Abandoned?) _____

Does Harry have a royal blood line? Does he have any relation to any dog
that ever lived in Buckingham Palace? _____

Has the Queen ever petted Harry? _____

Has Harry ever run through the legs of a public official? _____

Create your own Brand Plan and let your mind wander.

PERSONAL BRAND DOS AND DON'TS

The building phase is critical. Here are some dos and don'ts for building Harry's personal brand.

DOS

Use social media in a positive and professional way.

Share the right amount of info about your Adorable.

Use accessories to support your brand— sporty Harry needs to look sporty so invest in a backpack, googles, collar, etc., to make him look the part.

Adhere to the Rules of Pettiquette. (See Chapter 10 for more on Pettiquette and shaping your Adorable's character.)

Three Signs Harry has c

1. **He is trusted and known for his consistent and predictable behavior**

   Example: He will always chse squirrels and will always be known for his deep understanding of the limitations of dogs versus squirrels and how to not let it affect his positive mental attitude

2. **He passes the google test**

   Example: When you Google Harry the Adorable, content that showcases his skateboarding and surfing capabilities shows uo

ealthy Personal Brand

3. He stands out and is known for something specific

Example: Harry's ability to do the two step and garner a handlebar mustache makes him unique, and all of this many late-night show appearances have done an equally good job of drilling it into people's mind through repetition and consistency. Harry will stand out from thousands of others out there and the influencer opportunities that will come his way (dip, boots, and big hats) are perfectly aligned with his unique skills and interests.

DON'TS

Rants about the failures of the volunteers at the dog park to keep it clean or rants about any person or dog, for that matter. It is common knowledge that Harry's paws are not meant for typing but he still needs to avoid typos and bad grammar.

Sharing too much tedious trivia is just as bad as sharing too little. A day is long; not all of it needs to be shared—maintain the intrigue. Tedious items include household chores, work-related posts, and anything that the general public also has to do and doesn't particularly want to relive. "Behind the scenes" is a popular post but just because you are exposing your life it does not have to be the mundane part or too much of it. For example, a short clip of a bath is fun "behind the scenes," while you do a brand exposé on your favorite shampoo and describe why you love it, but is very different than filming the entire bath time, during which your Adorable turns your house into a mud cave.

Sporty Harry? Ditch the bow tie collar on the surfboard. Bow ties could be a danger to even the most sporty of canine; moreover, they are distracting and cumbersome. Consider what accessories you would wear as a sporty person and outfit your pal with the same.

Peeing on someone's picnic at the park will not support any brand, whereas greeting a new person nicely will cause an immediate positive first impression. An Adorable's brand is how they act and behave too.

CHAPTER 5

BEAUTIFUL INSIDE AND OUT: STELLAR ACCESSORIES FOR LIVING THE NARRATIVE

Historians have speculated that Adorables are so-called partly because of their savvy ability to accessorize. Not so. Adorables are adorable regardless of their fashion sense. However, when they do decide to accessorize it had better be on a par with their Adorable status. A well-intentioned wardrobe selection that does not heed the following unspoken rules of doggie fashion could undermine the irresistibility of an Adorable. If you choose this fun and dangerous path, here are some of the criteria that must be met.

Quality. Adorable clothes are well made and include items on labels and advertising with such words as Made in America, Craft, Made with Love, and Handmade.

Coordination. There is a great variety of accessories to coordinate including color, pattern, and theme. Like a daily shower for some, the theme can inadvertently be overlooked but is essential, nonetheless. Think of the horror of a plain nylon leash intermingled with a couture-themed collar or harness and poop bag holder. It does not work and is offensive to the label (and your Adorable).

Humiliation-Free. If your dog gets a strained look in his eye and a yearning to run for the hills, then the outfit or accessory selection does not contribute to adorableness. It detracts from it. Humiliation should be left to the object of your pranks not projected onto your Adorable. Runaway dogs, for the most part, have left due to humiliation combined with a gate being left open.

Safety. Flammability and off-gassing (from the fabric, not your Adorable) are primary safety concerns. These are both prevalent in synthetic fabric and plastics. Think of the new raincoat smell and then try and avoid it. If you have to consider whether your Adorable will go up in flames if someone else lights up, it likely has a high flammability rating. This may be an acceptable risk for a special occasion if your Adorable has had hours of "stop, drop, and roll" training.

SUMMER WEAR

Adorables could not let this season go by without a wardrobe response all their own.

Collar or harness. Can be padded and printed. Available in a dizzying array of options from leather, vegan leather, nylon with spikes, and adorned with gems. If Adorables are open to a summer switch-up collars are the perfect opportunity to integrate a cheery summer motif. Winter collars also exist.

Leash. Color and style will be driven by the collar selection but here again there are many options to integrate uplifting summer motifs. It may also be necessary to switch to a more durable option in the event of summer adventures or for the appearance of a pending one. Winter leashes also exist.

Bandana. Embrace the season with a summer-themed bandana that coordinates with your attire and your Adorable's collar and leash. Keep multiple options available for every day of the week, much like your grandmother's weekly pill organizer. Bandanas are loved for their versatility as you can pop one on your Adorable at any time for quick photo. They also provide a little variety and seasonal interest in your feed. Winter bandanas also exist.

Running harness. Statistically, outdoor activity, especially those requiring a running harness and leash, is done more often during the summer months. This handy invention may serve as a pulling harness when you tire as well. Your Adorable may even turn out to be a natural-born sled dog. Summer running harnesses can be used in fall and spring.

T-shirt. Time to turn the heavier winter outerwear in but if you are intent on apparel for your Adorable a lighter weight fabric in the form of a t-shirt will be more appropriate. Often printed in cute sayings like, "I Love my Mom" or "I'm a Talking Dog...Don't Ask," they're sure to garner an "Aww."

Backpack (human). Like the running harness, backpacks tend to be summer attire since opportunities for outdoor adventure, urban and remote, beckon more in the warmer months. When the adventure must go on but the little one's feet are "barkin'" then backpacks are the perfect place to take a load off. Not to mention there have been many a viral post of adorable heads popping out from the pack. May be used in fall or winter.

@oliverfreeride FOLLOW ...

143 likes

When the feet are barkin!

Backpack (doggie). Some are carried and others carry. If your adventure is such that gear transport is necessary, the sturdier Adorables can take on some of this burden by carrying a backpack. Mixer and a flask of whiskey can all be stowed for later indulgence. The trick is not to put your Adorable's own indulgences, such as his treats, in the backpack for fear he will disappear, returning only after his treat fix—in sharp contrast to the most successful of the marshmallow tests in 1972.[4]

Booties. Booties have the dual purpose of protecting both the delicate paws of your pup and your own home from the elements. When it comes to protecting your home a quick wipe at the door may be easier than on and offing booties but some think otherwise. So be it. The elements of the most adventurous include snowy explorations, volcanic rock (familiar to anyone who has tried to enjoy a lovely vacation beach side in Kona Hawaii), or the hot surfaces of the high desert.

Bow tie. Aside from unleashing the James Bond in your Adorable, the bow tie wearer exudes class and sophistication, a true fashion daredevil. To avoid danger ensure that your Adorable will not be doing any James Bond-like activities. The perfect summer bow tie can instantly transform your Adorable to a dog that has settled into summer with confidence and quirkiness.

WEATHER WEAR

Once thought of as the last layer required to face the elements. The wearable offerings have become more varied and are no longer considered solely to provide warmth and protection but instead comfort and fodder for your Insta feed.

Raincoat. Rubber-coated or vinyl suit Adorables that are most at home on

---

4   In 1972, a Stanford professor named Walter Mischel began conducting a series of important psychological studies. During his experiments, Mischel and his team tested hundreds of children—most of them around four and five years old. A child was offered a choice between one small but immediate reward, or two small rewards if they waited for a period of time. During this time, the researcher left the room for about 15 minutes and then returned. The point was to assess if the children could delay gratification. Researchers have made a lot this study and have exclaimed for years that this series of experiments proved that the ability to delay gratification was critical for success in life. However, no similar study has been conducted on dogs and therefore we should not assume the same conclusions would be reached.

a sailboat as first mates in a storm but are more often seen on damp urban walks. It either says, "I am the dog with all the cool stuff," or "I really stink when I get wet." Most desired in bright yellow.

Sweater. Sweaters are a large part of all dog personas and a wardrobe staple with multiple options for holiday wear; think ugly Christmas sweater, everyday wear like a Norwegian classic, or the softest cashmere. Some Adorables' sweater collections are known to make a regular human turn to jelly. Lighted sweaters are cute for your crazy aunt and uncle but will cause your pet humiliation, so keep your gates locked.

Hoodie. The only word to describe a hoodie is cute. A diverse wearable: black for the tough guy, grey casual or sports-themed for the active, and velour for the more refined. Adorables are taking back the hoodie and its endless options once thought to be hijacked by the Mark Zuckerberg set. Note that Adorables with extra-long fur around the eyes could be inadvertently injured in numerous ways if allowed to roam with a dark colored hoodie.

@harryandbalou

Comfort is what I live for!

Puffer jacket. Preferably lightweight like those popularized by Patagonia. You should look for qualities like rip stop material and material that snowflakes glance off. Exceptionally functional especially for those that wear it in any inclement weather but like a Patagonia, it works either way. A chubbier pup may rebel against this outfit for obvious reasons.

Reflective vest. With this vest you will be able to draw attention to your Adorable for safety reasons, and not just because he is adorable. The fact that he has one is a sure sign that you both have an upcoming adventure. For maximum content media opportunities, have your Adorable walk with kindergartners to school. He will look like a brave

WHAT WAS WITH THE NECK BARREL? CAN MY DOG HAVE ONE?

Your pal is very capable of carrying your stuff. Whether you consider him reliable with certain items is up to you and will depend on the item. Saint Bernards had the useful task of taking brandy to their rescued owners in the high Alps, or so we thought.

This was actually a story made up by a 17-year-old, but was such a good idea that it captured the imagination. At this point the world seems to be dumped on its head and items like the Kurgo flask, which we are tasked with carrying to support our pets' hydration needs, seem to have won over the neck barrel concept.

To calculate the size of the barrel, take the length of the dog, and the width of the dog and buy a barrel smaller than either.

protector and crossing guard even if children aren't his favorite.

Neoprene vest. Heavy-duty camo evokes immediate thoughts of your dog's obedience, purpose, and skill. For the serious outdoor dog, it should come complete with padded chest protection to protect your Adorable from sticks and brush. Not available in mini poodle size.

Sleepwear. The favorite choice of attire for the most endearing photographs. Think robe, in bed, with sleeping mask nearby. Sleepwear can be in the form of a jumper, cotton vest, or cushy robe. Like a chamomile tea at bedtime, doggie sleepwear gets you and your Adorable in the chill frame of mind. A robe in reverse, is a Snuggie.

YOUR ADORABLE'S COLLAR

The options are endless for those who want to go beyond the practical and express their Adorable's personality (or desired personality) with a collar. Classifying dogs by their collars is nothing new; the most ornate dog collars belonged to the dogs of nobles as far back as 209 BC.

Plain nylon. For the unassuming and bath time. Sturdy, easy to wear, replaceable, and in a range of colors with matching lead.

Leather. Sturdy, practical, long wearing. All-purpose plain or stamped with unassuming leatherwork.

Jeweled. May involve a sacrifice for fashion in the form of rough edges and a dent in your pocketbook.

Nylon with fabric overlay. Practical yet personal options abound. Dog named Tugboat? Cute little tugboats can adorn your collar. When someone looks confused after you introduce your dog, the collar motif may help them with a tough name.

Leather and spikes. Screams "I am tough," or the reverse, with intended irony. If kept clean enough can be moved into your own repertoire for a sultry evening.

Chain. Circa 1980s training method and reserved for those not bothered by choking and hissing sounds from a closed-off windpipe.

WHERE TO SHOP?

One of the burdens that Adorables must bear is that they cannot just buy their clothes in any brick-and-mortar store or shop or mass online marketplace. Luckily, a new crop of direct-to-consumer shopping options with cutting-edge styles and at premium quality make it easy for an Adorable to switch from sun to freezing temperatures and day to evening wear without skipping a beat.

Of course, each Adorable persona has some manifestations that are unique and there is an online and sometimes an offline store that caters to everything. For instance, for the active, there are stores with gear brought to you by law enforcement families and outdoor enthusiasts who understand your precise plight; for the fashionista there are high fashion options from top labels or indie brands that were trained by the top labels but ventured out to make their mark in dog couture. Each is self-aware and due to the magnificent search capabilities of Google both worlds are at your fingertips. If you still find yourself coming up with only dresses when you were searching for a backpack here is a handy guide that will see you through such an emergency.

ACTIVES AND ACTIVE-ASPIRING

Tactipup. Handmade goods procured within the US with a focus on quality are right up the alley of an Adorable that means business and doesn't want to mess around with returns. Big sellers are custom patches that can be applied to collars and harnesses with your pet's name on a camo background or even regular, in-stock badges that proclaim Service Dog. tactipup.com.

Ruffwear. This brand claims to induce an infectious passion for inspiring exploration in outdoor adventurers and their human companions. Popular with those dreaming of their next adventure, they are often sighted on the trail and riverfront (except for the booties, which have also regularly been spotted on some downtown Los Angeles Adorables). Ruffwear.com.

Kurgo. The birthplace of the high-quality running belt with various leash attachments. Dedicated site sections with offerings for your sport of choice. Kurgo claims it is committed to companionship, enabling people and dogs to get outside and confidently explore their worlds together. For those not confident before, perhaps the bowls, packs, booties, and first aid kit will put the "I can" in your outdoor repertoire. Kurgo.com.

FASHIONISTA

Hermès, Gucci, and Louis Vuitton all stepped into the pet fashion market in various ways, from dog collars to carriers. For the label-loving fashionista, being among the first to take up these offerings will be a mandate.

However, if you are looking for something more individual with a less established cache, here are some alternatives.

Rororiri. Former apprentice under the designer Peter Som, Rita Li founded Rororiri. Known for bow ties and dog jackets, the Eva cardigan, an adorable take on Chanel's classic tweed jacket, has been seen getting some swooning attention around outdoor cafés of Manhattan (it was the Adorable getting the attention, but eyes were initially drawn to the Eva). rororiri.com.

Muttropolis. You can fill your cart with selections of shirts, pajamas, costumes, dresses, accessories, sweaters, and jackets and then head over to the Collections offerings and click on a featured collection to satisfy your label-loving itch with their cheeky dog-friendly takes on Louis Vuitton, Chanel, and Hermès. Muttropolis.com.

BAG REVEAL OF THE AVERAGE WOMAN DOG OWNER

More is more and most of it has a purpose.

1. Bag. Size may match the size of the dog.

2. Phone. This lifeline should remain in hand rather than in the purse to avoid any delay in obtaining daily captures, responding to comments and DMs, and communicating with brands and partners on the go. Digging around in your bag while Harry is doing a handstand is way too frustrating.

3. Doggie water bottle. Knowing that everyone needs water on the go, your Adorable's water bottle with water bowl top is always in the bag but somehow, despite this knowledge, your own water bottle, not so much.

4. Dog treats. A must-have if your Adorable requires an immediate reward for doing something extra adorable or to be coaxed into something.

5. Poop bag in stylish holder. May also be attached to leash so you are never without or have to backtrack to where you left your bag to play with your pup and catch a serious stink-eye from a disgruntled citizen self-appointed to poop patrol while you are trying to procure a poop bag.

6. Leash (in hand or in bag). Another item that may remain in bag if accessible but more likely in hand unless your dog is also in bag.

7. Lint roller. Most times a little hair is ignored but if you have something important to do after a cuddle you may need it.

8. Wipes. Paws, eyes, slobber on you or your dog.

9. New tennis ball. Once used or wet does not get thrown back in bag. Instead, is gently carried between forefinger and thumb. Usually accompanied by a chuck-it.

10. Lip oil. Addictive. Rejuvenate lips exposed to the elements and restore a healthy glow with antioxidants.

11. Wallet (one edge may have a chew mark).

12. AirPods. Allows for hands-free discussions so both hands can be applied to leash if a squirrel goes by.

13. Extra phone battery. Invaluable if you get stuck chatting to your mother at the dog park and don't have enough charge for your next meeting.

14. Make-up. For impromptu meet-ups or touch-ups. Sometimes there may be Adorable humans, and not just Adorable dogs out and about, who may cause you to want to spruce up.

15. Perfume. Fresh and clean is welcome and avoids confusion around which of you needs a bath.

16. Business cards. Just in case you meet that perfect dog walker or house sitter while out and about and want him or her to have your digits.

17. Coins. Thrown slyly into any fountain to avoid Harry thinking it was a ball and using the fountain as a pond. Each throw is accompanied by a wish for Harry's good health and happiness.

TOP SIX OUTFIT THEMES TO AVOID

Those with the power to press the "buy" button on behalf of their Adorables take great pleasure in pressing it with what appears, at times, to be impaired judgment. This is not just the incorrect sizing purchases they consistently make for themselves; these purchases are more inappropriate than the bride wearing white at wedding number 10. There is a fine line between tasteful and hilarious; between cute and outright inappropriate and sad.

If you want to keep your dog from being humiliated and have him maintain his Adorable status, train those fingers to not press the "Buy" button on these following trends:

1. Fetish-like Apparel

    Perhaps well-meaning but no Adorable needs to put the "pet" in petish (in fact, let's just remove "petish" from use altogether). The only outcome of putting fetish-like outfits on your pet will be to inspire awkward and conflicting emotions in canine and human alike. Some of these looks are adopted by young women at costume parties as a straight-faced excuse to show extra skin. Although they may work in that context, it is highly doubtful that your dog will be proud of himself with this look. The only thing worse than the initial selection is a matching set for the owner and the awkward excitement or confusion from bystanders that will likely follow.

2. Child Fantasy Characters

    Think Tooth Fairy, Santa Claus, and the Easter Bunny. Or any other magical character who brings you free stuff. These childhood fantasy characters are meant to bring us joy through their jolly natures and gifts left behind, not sadness and pity.

    If your dog does not chew the outfit to bits, then you will be constantly adjusting it after he repeatedly tries wiping off the sartorial embarrassment on any nearby object as he would a good perfume.

3. Edible Items

No one should be imagining their Adorable as a food item on a plate or menu. Whether it's a hot dog, sushi, taco, or cookie costume, we must all remember that despite your Adorable sleeping in your bed, he does have predators (in some cultures even consisting of humans). Add to that the plain and simple humiliation and there is nothing more certain than ridiculous food items as dog clothing should be bypassed.

4. Human Attire

Many things can spur on the desire to dress your dog in people clothes that people themselves hate wearing. Whether it's a doggy wedding, your IG feed, or a holiday don't make your pet wear a tux at your wedding when you are in flip flops and a Hawaiian shirt.

Just imagine if you had to wear something like this (oh you did, and you quit your job as a result because it was too tight, movement-restraining, and scratchy). Most outfits also require adding an extra set of creepy arms to their four-limbed body. No thumbs but six limbs are not helpful, and no mammal comes similarly equipped.

He knows it's wrong, as sure as he knows wet food is better than dry and balls must be chased. He knows that those he trusted and gave unconditional love to are judging and amused at his expense.

Note: This is general guidance. There are some Adorables that can don human attire without humiliation like @menswear but it is not typical.

5. Other Animals

As said by the worldly and wise: To bee or not to bee? That is the question.

Actually, it's not a question for your Adorable, because the answer will always be no. Your Adorable is the most superior animal in existence and one of the worst things you can dress him up in is another animal.

Your Adorable is likely already confused as to whether or not he qualifies as a human; now you are adding to his confusion by dressing him in animal outfits. This includes putting him in leopard print. Save him from his misery and avoid these outfits like fleas.

6. Space or AstroNOT Attire

    Remember Laika, a mixed-breed dog that was launched on the Soviet Union's Sputnik 2 mission in November 1957 and was the first living being in orbit? She was an unintended hero and chosen for this perilous mission exactly because she was unable to object to being put in such a dangerous situation. Also, remember that horrible cone your Adorable had to wear when he hurt his foot? If ever there was an opportunity for puppy trauma, here it is.

    Your Adorable does not want to consider the potentially fateful activity of space flight, nor does he want to wear a cone like collar around his neck. Therefore, there is no reason to subject him to an embarrassing astronaut costume.

CHAPTER 6

THE ADORABLE DIET: NUTRITION TIPS FOR BETTER SMELLS, HEALTH, AND LOOKS

Adorables, as a group, consider nutrition to be at the top of the list for looking and feeling good. Their discriminating nature drives most nutritional decisions but at times the tastiest is not always the best for appearance and odor. Adorables are also driven by the same considerations as Ghandi, who provided such insight as, "It is health that is real wealth and not pieces of gold or silver." For an Adorable, however, gold and silver do follow good health: there is a direct correlation between sound nutrition and manifestations of good health in appearance, which for an Adorable may lead to gold.

Pet food companies have been accused of trickery by fueling human emotions around the appropriate diet for Adorables, a deception that has become more controversial than Alaska's Bridge to Nowhere and just as revealing of common underhand tactics. Nevertheless, pet food and the act of feeding your Adorable, a seemingly simple biological necessity, is

DIET
DOPPELGANGING

Sue & Bartholomew

John & Milo

complicated and entangled with different emotions, ideas, memories, and rituals, which deserve to be unpacked.

DIET DOGPEGÄNGING.

Those responsible for the diet of Adorables are sometimes misguided when it comes to the nutritional needs of their dog—an extension of doppel-gänger concept[5] (discussed further in Chapter 13 in reference to looka-like Adorables). Many Adorables' diets inadvertently become reflections of their charge's diet or what their charge desires their diet to be regardless of their or their Adorable's actual nutritional needs. Like Bartholomew, Milo, Luvy, Tony, and Merle, who became distinct dogpelgängers of their charges, at least from the perspective of their diets.

SUE & BARTHOLOMEW

Sue lives by the mantra, "once on the lips, forever on the hips," and is dedicated to her health and wellbeing though calorie counting. When her calorie allocation is up for the day, as indicated on her Noom app, she may find herself in a state of hunger, but she has learned that even though her natural inclination is to place food items in hand she receives the same amount of satisfaction by quickly diverting the snack to Bartholomew upon its approach to her lips.

Bartholomew is not a dogpelgänger in the traditional sense, since Sue does not have a belly that drags on the floor, however, she probably would have if it were not so detrimental to her health and her modeling career. Sue's Adorable dachshund gets only short walks as his own belly does drag on the floor and although he needs to watch what goes down his trap, unfor-

---

5   Doppelgänger, meaning literally a double of a living person. The word "doppelgänger" or dogpelgänger is often used in a more general and neutral sense, and in slang, to describe any dog who resembles a person, or person that resembles another person.

tunately many items meant for Sue's mouth end up in his, so he tends to run a consistent 7–10 pounds heavy despite switches to various "diet" dog foods. Sue is an expert at watching her calories so aside from the many snacks throughout the day, Sue and Bartholomew share very similar, strictly proportioned, low-calorie mealtime fare.

JOHN & MILO

John was relegated to the husky sizing model from a young age and has been on various diet and exercise programs throughout his life, overseen by a serious certified trainer. John tends to yo-yo in clothing sizes and has been committed to his health and fitness for the last 10 years but lives in fear of a regression that sometimes causes sleep issues. John's kitchen counter is adorned with a food scale, Ninja blender, and an espresso machine. The demands of organizing Milo's nutritional needs along with his own was too much and therefore John utilizes a raw food subscription model that supplies pre-packaged meals to a precise nutritional optimum mix certified by AFFCO.[6] He worries, though, that Milo may need additional support and when making his morning smoothie shares his greens with Milo.

John's lab, Milo, is also on a strict diet to maintain weight and is fed at to-the-minute feeding times with optimum nutrition of venison and buffalo in carefully calibrated blends of protein, grains, and fats. No people food allowed for this pooch and treats are doled out with the same control as exhibited by nuns overseeing an orphanage even though Milo is more than deserving throughout the day. Needless to say, he is in optimum health, has not struggled with obesity like his counterparts, and has a love for greens and a very shiny coat. Despite Milo's ordinarily cheery disposition he sometimes mopes about John's house with a certain yearning for a little leftover lean turkey and on his walks regularly tips over trash cans looking for anything that might taste good.

MARGARET & LUVY

Margaret is the grandmother adored by all (especially kids) but known to frustrate parents. Although kids love to visit Margaret, their parents dread them due to the candy jars stationed for free feeding throughout her house and multiple ice cream parties held during each visit. Inevitably, upon their arrival back home all household items become a trampoline. Margaret's most oft asked question, both to people and to her Adorable, Luvy, is, "Are you hungry?" Margaret herself maintains her own weight perfectly and does not have any difficulty with overindulging, while those around

---

6   The Association of American Feed Control Officials (AAFCO) has been around since September 1906 with the longstanding purpose to serve as a venue for feed regulators to explore the problems encountered in administering feed laws; to develop just and equitable standards, definitions and policies for the enforcement of feed laws; and to promote uniformity in laws, regulations and enforcement policies. AAFCO has created a large number of models providing guidance, definitions, terms and best-management practices in addition to the Model Bill and Model Feed Regulations (including Model Pet Food Regulations). Governmental agencies of North America who enforce animal-feed regulations, including those for pet food do this with the support of AAFCO.

her have waistlines that typically expand as they lose control from sugar overdoses.

Luvy, a miniature poodle, eats more treats than regular meals and is constantly advised by the vet to slim down for health reasons. Luvy doppelgängs Margaret, not with treats but with her cute face. Luvy is an expert in "cute face" as any time she nears a human (cute or not) she is rewarded with a treat. Obedience commands confuse Luvy as she is not typically expected to summon that much effort to get a treat. Despite Luvy's consistent diet of treats she still enjoys table scraps from Margaret's leftovers. Margaret has had to take Luvy to the vet monthly for alternating cases of bowel issues and being unable to keep food down: she barfs more than she barks (which is not part of the doppelgänger theory as it pertains to this pair since Margaret has no such ailment). The jury is still out on the cause of the issues.

RAMÓN & TONY

Ramón works hard and plays hard but for him, playing hard is not a night on the town filled with raucous japes but a game (or several) of Fortnite with his Adorable and a couple of brews. Ramón has a belly that makes shoe tying tricky but has accepted his new form, adapted, and simply bought slip-ons. Ramón shares most meals with his Adorable, Tony, which are likely fast food. He also has a tendency to overfeed the kibble when he feels guilty for cutting his walk short to fit in another game of Fortnite. Ramón has not really caught on to the "whole food" phenomena, either for himself or Tony. He has created his own food desert; he selects Tony's food based on price and availability at the corner store while his own is based on taste and availability at the same corner store.

Tony, an overweight pitbull cross, has worked a dent in the couch where he spends a lot of time with his pal sitting way too close to the 76-inch TV. He enjoys his kibble and is perfectly content with the extra feedings in lieu of walks but gets sad when others note his strong odor, likely derived from his tasty but brightly (artificially) colored food. Tony has developed some vision problems and regularly walks into door frames. On a recent walk, Tony pegged the needle reading of a Geiger counter when passing a local Army surplus store.

MELANIE & MERLE

Melanie is a sleek and confirmed track star who holds the current junior national record for the 400m hurdles (women's 400m hurdle races require the hurdler to possess the speed of a sprinter and the ability to clear 10 barriers, each 36 inches high). As such she focuses on her training regimen more than Michael Phelps (minus the five-egg breakfast omelet). To be at her best she needs to plan her food intake like a jockey on the eve of the Kentucky Derby. Her sleek, hyena-like stature is often admired by others as is her pronounced bone structure, resulting from her dedication to her sport rather than genetics. Melanie spends countless hours balancing carb/fat ratios and planning her workouts for her cause.

Merle, Melanie's whippet, is as sleek as they come and is offered top quality food in the same carb/fat proportions that Melanie attributes to getting herself to where she is at. He has no similar upcoming hurdle events but, like Michael Phelps, though not in a pool, often burns several thousand calories a day due to frigid temperatures (even in a down coat provided by Melanie) and running very fast. Merle's sleek, hyena-like stature, which Melanie considers normal and part of the breed, would make him a top hurdler but alas the closest AKC event is agility, which he has refused to do. These same attributes have also been noticed in Merle #2 through #8.

PET HERO
SUSAN THIXTON, THE CAPED CRUSADER FOR PET FOOD

Susan runs the site TruthaboutPetFood.com hoping to share information she learns about pet food with others and advocating for safe pet food. Her zest for the rights of Adorables is commendable.

Susan is known for declaring, "True justice is enforcement of law…the true interest of the pet-owning public is safe pet foods free of diseased animals and animals that have died other than by slaughter. We will continue to fight for our pets…**this isn't over.**"

Susan prepares a regularly updated list of pet foods she would (and does) trust to give to her own pets, which is available to purchase through her website.

LABELS AND INGREDIENTS
IN THE PET FOOD WORLD—A TRANSLATION

Not only is the pet food world fraught with confusing terminology but pet food itself also contains a dizzying number of creative claims thought to be developed by a herd of interns on a quest for corporate recognition. Here is a handy guide for interpreting some of what you may see on your dog food label.

Artisanal. The common dictionary definition is food that is produced in limited quantities by artisans using traditional methods. In the ancient languages it is translated as, "a way to charge more for the same thing." The proprietors of dog food offered for commercial sale seem to not be the type to hire artisans and produce in limited quantities as this would present a serious economic challenge, so this begs the questions: What does this mean to your Adorable? And why is it on pet food?

Freeze-dried. Food preparation that removes moisture content to make it shelf stable. More expensive than regular heat processing, though it's unclear if freeze-drying produces greater nutritional benefits. Freeze-dried food will still be edible when scientists know the answer to whether or not cryogenics actually works.

Gourmet. If gourmet conjures images of a chef hat you are consistent with Merriam Webster's definition of the term, which is, "of, relating to, or being high quality, expensive, or specialty food typically requiring expert preparation." Sounds great but it's unclear how it adds to the food experience of your dog, who would likely rather chase down a gopher and eat it raw. One leading pet food brand attempted to sell Gourmet Prey Raw Gopher, but difficulties in maintaining a consistent supply chain and consumers' ability to see through the rouse led to a massive brand failure.

Human Grade. Think if you miss a trip to the grocery store that you can nip into your Adorable's food cupboard and steal a pouch just because it declares itself human grade? This term has no definition in any animal feed regulations; it is still best to steer clear of your Adorable's food even with a proclamation of "human grade."

Raw Dog Food. Sometimes raw means delivered to you raw and in an uncooked state and sometimes it means that prior to cooking it was in a raw state, which would describe most food on the planet. Certain dog food brands appear to have empowered the interns too much. An example from one popular pet food brand of this: "Our mission represents a new standard in pet food, designed to nourish dogs and cats…using ingredients that are sustainable and harvested by regional suppliers, delivered to our kitchen FRESH or RAW." The use of "or" is particularly concerning. To clarify what this means in relatable terms, would you be more likely to watch the *FRESH Prince of Bel Air*, or the *RAW Prince of Bel Air*? The correct answer is neither.

Dyes and coloring. It seems that the least expensive dog food correlates with the brightest color offerings. Red 40, Yellow 5, and Yellow 6, for example, have been found to be carcinogenic but have at least now been banned in Europe for human consumption. Note that certain shades of red are a product of a bug concoction that so far only Starbucks has had legal trouble with for stating its products are vegan. The vegans among us took issue with consuming ground up bugs but your Adorable may not.

Prey Foods. Certain pet foods have introduced "prey" lines stating: "In the wild, the diet of the canine or feline was simpler, consisting primarily of the prey they hunted. That's why we created Taste of the Wild Prey Limited Ingredient Diet—a simplified approach to pet food based on the protein sources of your animal's native diet." A large Angus cow on the front of the bag *should* conjure up an image of your Adorable, currently lounging on the sofa, taking down a cow in the wild. But wait, you think, are there really cows in the wild and would my dog hunt one? Is this wild prey food filled with mice, moths, and crickets too, which are technically wild prey (after all, the food chain is a complex structure)? If it isn't, then attempt to forget the whole thing.

Prescription Diet. An unregulated marketing term, which usually means you have to purchase the products through your vet. No prescription is required to buy these foods, nor do they have to meet any special requirements or get approval from the FDA or other regulatory body. If you find yourself considering the need for some "prescription dog food," take a piece of paper, write down what you want, and then scribble an unintelligible signature akin to what any vet would do before then going shopping for quality dog food.

PET HERO
MARY STRAUS

Mary created DogAware.com to help people to make the best decisions for their dogs. It is designed for people who like to ask questions and understand the reasoning behind decisions. The number one guidance on the site is to keep your questions relevant to dogs and not your personal relationships.

Signs Your Pet Food Could Use and Upgrade

SIGNS YOUR PET CAN USE A FOOD UPGRADE

Poor quality pet food is to blame for some serious health issues including heart disease, diabetes, and allergies. Before these conditions strike you may first see these more obvious signs of poor nutrition.

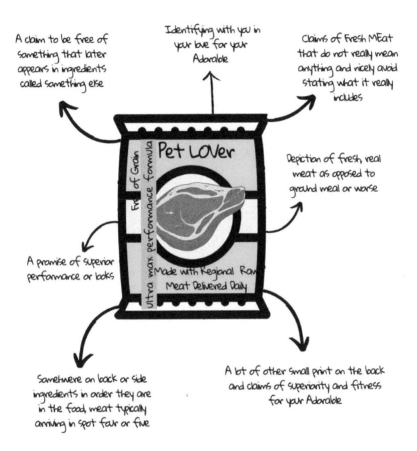

Anatomy of a Dog Food Bag

A claim to be free of something that later appears in ingredients called something else

Identifying with you in your love for your Adorable

Claims of Fresh MEat that do not really mean anything and nicely avoid stating what it really includes

Depiction of fresh, real meat as opposed to ground meal or worse

A promise of superior performance or looks

Somewhere on back or side ingredients in order they are in the food, meat typically arriving in spot four or five

A lot of other small print on the back and claims of superiority and fitness for your Adorable

Pet LOVer

Free of Grain

Ultra max performance formula

Made with Regional Raw Meat Delivered Daily

THE PET FOOD BAG

Product buying decisions are typically made from the information contained on the front panel of a product, referred to as the principal panel. In the dog food world these decisions can be tricky to navigate and packages often have more real estate bias for lovely meaty imagery, while the true nutritional content is usually in micro-sized font somewhere on the back. To avoid hours in the grocery aisle with a magnifying glass, here is your guide to a typical dog food bag.

Typical Adorable Diet

Special Pupsicle or Dog Beer While Haning with Pal

Dog Bones and other Large Chewables to Curb Boredom

Dog Treats Reward for Learning New Skill

Smaller Dog Treats Reward for Being Amazing

Dog Treats Reward for Being Adorable

Proper Nutritionally Balanced Dog Food plus Supplements

TREATS

Adorables are used to treats, a lot of treats. They usually deserve them for their stellar obedience or as a token of your love. They are also a great way to have them love you even if you're not very likable or have scary teeth.

Doggone Easy Snowcones

1 Puree your dog-friendly fresh or frozen fruit or veggies.

If using veggies, make sure they are cooked first. For the most Likes and the best-looking snow cone, think colors — like raspberries, watermelon, carrots, pumpkin mixture, or peas.

2 Add chicken stock or water to your puree to thin the mixture and then add crushed ice.

3

Enjoy!

HOMEMADE TREATS

If you find that your fingers are often at the bottom of the treat jar and you are having difficulty keeping a supply in stock, making treats from scratch may be the way to go. The extra effort will not only show a special kind of love but also provide a constant source of ammunition to keep your Adorable behaving the way you want. Added bonus: treats can be customized for the season in picture-worthy shapes and flavors and made in large batches, much like your IG content, referred to by some as "batching."

Picture this rolling through your feed: your Adorable and you each enjoying a refreshing treat poolside. When it starts to heat up pupsicles are preferred to ice cream, which may rock his delicate Adorable system.

CBD CALLING?

Cannabidiol (or CBD) is the centerpiece of upgraded wellness for Adorables. Humans are loving it and the benefits are equally transferrable to our four-legged friends. For some, it's like a glass of wine at the end of a long day with only the benefits and no hangover; for others it has the pain relief characteristics of an aspirin but not the liver-damaging effects.

There is some question as to what makes the perfect CBD supplement: is it an oil-based tincture, spray, or a treat? Effectiveness is a must and for that you need a version that will get through the body and be absorbed, which means a water-soluble hemp concentrate, like Calm from Madrigal Creatives.

If you're not sure it'll work just remember that dogs and cats used to hunt CBD in the wild and if turned loose in a hemp field would very much enjoy themselves.

FOODS TO AVOID TO PREVENT INEVITABLE ODORS

If your Adorable is not sweet smelling they may not be as irresistible as they should be. You may have unfairly blamed your Adorable for a certain smell once or twice but more often than not your Adorable will always have been responsible for malodorous air. Unlike the eponymous character in *Walter the Farting Dog*, whose superpower is farting and who is capable of fending off robbers with his farts, the more typical refrain is, "Good Lord, what could have caused that? There must be something seriously wrong."

Some odors can be caused by a serious underlying problem, but most have a simple solution and may be the result of ingesting the following known odor-causing offenders:

You can track whether it's your dog and what you've been feeding him that's causing bad odors using a handy chart that, until now, was coveted by vets and guarded with utmost secrecy.

Go easy adding cauliflower (which should be cooked), cauliflower may be referred to as a gas mushroom cloud.*

With pinto, black, butter, or red kidney beans less is more if your pooch has a history of gassy stomachs.*

Brussel sprouts are known as 'little round gas balls' for good reason. These nutritious balls of goodness have a reputation for generating gas resulting in offensive flatulence.*

Cabbage is another gas-generating vegetable. If brussels sprouts are 'little round gas balls' cabbage is a large round gas ball.*

SMELL LEXICON

FOOD	SMELL
Purina Dog Chow	Rodent death
Top tier dog food	Rodent death and cow entrails with hint of freshly harvested cauliflower field
Chili con carne	Chili con carne
Scallops with lime juice	Beer
Homemade doggy treats	Love, floral with hints of cardamom, overlaid with cinnamon
Sticks and grass	Sticks and grass
Rib bones (absconded from tabletop)	No smell due to resulting stomach issues
Tofu	Tofu left in fridge past use by date

CHAPTER 7

A PERFECTLY-TAILORED HOME IS WHERE THE PERFECT ADORABLE IS

Experts say that it takes just 26 seconds for a guest to form an opinion of your home when they walk through the front door and that opinion is manifested upon you and those in your household.

To judge is inevitable and first impressions of your home count. If you want to create a great first impression of your dog, your house is the first step. Similar to the odds against you in Vegas, so too the many missteps that can occur in any visit to the home of an Adorable. Which is why there should be great emphasis on the home environment.

Your guest arrives, enticed by the promise of a new party trick. She is ready for fun and in a frame of mind to shower your beloved dog with attention.

However, if you have not taken the time to properly equip and dress your home, on her way into the living room a dog toy will get caught underfoot causing her to trip and fall. She'll land with her nose in a rug with the scent of wet dog clinging to it.

Sprawled on the floor face down, she'll turn her head to see a chewed piano bench leg that you were going to repair after you'd completed an online furniture repair class.

At this point, your dog's reputation is already soiled with everyone that your guest has ever direct messaged. Still, there's more humiliation to come.

Your guest stands up and asks where the bathroom is. She will return with an attitude.

So instead of spending the evening marveling at your precious, she is fastidious about washing her hands, avoids eye contact with your little love, and eats with her reading glasses on as she searches for dog hair in her salad.

At this point, even if your dog could recite poetry while juggling flaming knives, it would not reverse the damage done and put him back in the top 10 Adorables listings.

It does not have to be this way.

The dog and his needs can be integrated into a well-kept home, which can result in the perfect marriage of utility and excellence along with others' high opinions of you and your furry roommate. Sought after virtues are classic, well kept, handsome, and loved. Some décor essentials will help as, of course, will our handy guides.

DÉCOR DOS AND DÉCOR DON'TS

DOS	DON'TS
Upholstered pieces with heavy-duty fabric and great design..	Vinyl protectors.
Materials must repel. Durable flooring such as tile or concrete, and easy-wash surfaces. Mud does not show up as easily on lighter colors with texture. Favorites include tile with semi-dark grout.	Absorption is the enemy with flooring like wall-to-wall carpeting Steer clear of this dust mite playground.
Tasteful action prints of dogs.	Prints of dogs playing poker. Although ironic, also an eyesore, unless your pet has replaced one of the original gambling canines.
Sturdy floor lamps. Strong enough not to tip, but soft enough not to hurt hip (during lite play).	Floor lamps with tripod legs that can easily get caught up in bumping and humping.
Sturdy sofa with steel legs, like a Floyd Sofa.	Sofa with wooden legs—a beacon for power-chewers.
A high shelf for consistent remote-control storage.	A side table for remote control storage that inevitably has a few chew marks.
Low pile durable rugs like sisal that can be tossed without heartache when your pet or a visitors' pet has an accident.	An antique rug exported from Turkey on your last vacation that will make you sad and regret hauling it home when exposed to inevitable wear and tear of a dog and the occasional accident, or a high pile rug that holds stench and dirt. These are fine for use in a minivan.
Durable baskets for toy storage.	Toys strewn on the floor with small bits of exiting polyester stuffing that will get tripped over and choked on.
Stylish, easy-to-clean, and durable doggie placemats.	You or your kindergartner's laminated school project placemat made for a previous Thanksgiving that you've inevitably placed on a water-stained floor.

Stylish bowls in a holder (especially if you have a large dog).

A hook or small basket by the door to hang or place a leash.

A comfortable and stylish throw that can go on the couch for your dog to lie down on and be removed when guests arrive.

Sturdy pillows that can be thrown on the floor for play or a snuggle.

Non-textured walls that are easily wiped clean.

Outdoor dog sprayer.

Modern dog crate made of wood that doubles as a coffee table.

Stylish dog bed made with heavy-duty fabric. Its cover comes off for easy laundering and matches your décor.

Furniture for bounding. A one-hop jump and into the sky Super Dog goes. A confidence builder and a beautiful, shareable image.

DOG MOTIFS

A dog motif can be used judiciously to pledge your allegiance and reveal your love and commitment to your dog throughout the home. Not evidence that you have a dog, like a half-eaten remote control, rather something in the form of a pawprint, dog graphic, or a print of your favorite breed or breeds.

In many instances animated dog motifs with overly large eyes and hearts denoting love can bring about an instant and unconscious love for your star. However, subtlety and placement are critical as is having the dog motif arise in unexpected ways. A tasteful motif where least expected can be a charming addition to the design of any home and appreciated as an asset. Some ideas for carriers of the motif:

MAGNETS

SOUP TUREENS

POT WARMERS

DOORMATS

MAILBOXES

BOOKENDS

COASTERS

MUGS

BOXER SHORTS

BAR GLASSES

HATS

BAGS

ART
(ALL PHOTOS WILL NATURALLY
CONTAIN YOUR CURRENT DOG OR A
PREVIOUS ONE)

Stainless steel bowls that get tripped over and clang loudly whenever someone is sleeping, sometimes spilling food and always spilling water.

No dedicated hook or basket anywhere, which causes a mad search (like the daily search for your phone) whenever the dog needs to go out.

A throw with an extra-large image of you and your dog.

Small white pillows, cross stitched with "Home Is Where the Dog is," or a picture of your dog that inevitably gets confused with a dog toy.

Pawprint wallpaper.

Large laundry sink that causes you to put your back out while trying to lift dog into it to clean his paws.

Large unused plastic or wire dog crate in the middle of the living room that becomes an impromptu ottoman or coffee table.

Bright yellow dog bed that has a wet dog waft emanating from it and leaves a trail of polyester filling and dust when relocated or your dog gets bored.

Anything that could be mistaken for a tree or fire hydrant.

OPEN CONCEPT: A DOG IN YOUR SPACE

Dog gets snuggles here, dog waits for your arrival here, and dog serves as entertainment for all to love and adore here. The kitchen and living room are really the heart of the home, not that we need a cross-stich pillow identifying them as such.

Contrary to standard decorating advice that contains tips about hiding the fact that a dog lives in a home, a different approach is to celebrate the fact that you have a four-legged roommate provided it is done with judicious taste and durability. You obviously enjoy having your four-legged friend around so why not focus on casual comfort while also trying to maintain your love of neutrals? After all, no one wants to be washing slip covers

weekly (like most people who share a home with a dog!). Strive for rugged, clean, and comfortable, just like the comfy sofa for snuggling complete with one chewed leg from your Adorable's puppy years.

The following space says "versatility." At any given moment, you or your dog are comfortable, and all your needs can be met in any spot in the room.

1 Flat-screen TV. Its only use is to turn on a replay of Harry's favorite show while you are at work, otherwise remains unwatched, except for sports. If you can get Harry to wear a jersey, then any sporting event is a shareable moment.

2 Remote control with chew marks on side table.

3 Sisal rug, not so easy to clean but easy to toss out and replace.

4 Adorable pictures on the wall of you and your Adorable through the years doing adorable things.

5 Bookshelf with a few books (most are on the Kindle), e.g., *Wag, Dog Training Guide, A Dog's Purpose*. Note: *Wag the Dog* is not a pet movie.

6 Dog bookends procured from a trip to Europe, tastefully exhibiting the dog motif.

7 Large dog artwork.

8 Bar cart—dog heads on cocktail stirrers and pawprint coasters.

9 Jar full of organic treats with a bottle of Calm or Relieve Plus! to spray on treat to ensure a hemp-infused snack is always at the ready. These are loved for their ability to calm pets quickly.

10 Large sturdy basket under coffee table for dog toys (only soft toys and a kong are allowed in the house; no balls or ball throwers after the last flat screen incident).

11 Coffee table with steel legs. After the couch incident you got smart and purchased furniture with an eye to it withstanding your dog. Buy the table after your buddy has reached full size so you can gauge possible head and eye injuries.

12 Unused crate with custom cover from Etsy seller that you bought with good intentions; now in the corner with orthopedic dog bed inside.

13 Piano and padded bench for those adorable duets with your baying friend. Train for the "high C" note with treats placed on that key. For information on piano notes, please read Cesare Magdaloni's *The Art of Piano Keys and What they Do*.

14 Rug throw made of (synthetic) fur for coziness. Looks good and can still be thrown in the wash.

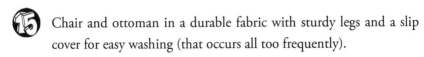

15. Chair and ottoman in a durable fabric with sturdy legs and a slip cover for easy washing (that occurs all too frequently).

16. Shelves with childhood dogs' ashes and collar.

17. Walls in semi-gloss paint: when the kong filled with peanut butter gets a good shaking and peanut butter ends up on the walls, they can easily wiped.

18. Puzzle feeder in the vain hope that dog will savor the pupscription dog food (you do not recall how to cancel it).

19. Large cannister to hold dog food while dog food bag yearns for a built-in to solve the issue. The cannister should have a paw release for Henry to grab a quick snack.

20. Pet bowl set over sturdy, stylish mat for easy cleanup and to stop floor damage resulting from constant water splashes.

21. Curtains, not blinds with strings for dog to get caught up in and use for tug-o-war.

22. Essential oil diffuser with lavender or orange scents to mask inevitable dog aroma that is undetectable to you when friends come over.

23. Dog toy for distraction, play, and entertainment as opposed to chewing something treasured.

24. Half-done custom puzzle with an image of Harry in his puppy years. Dogs are unable to solve a puzzle with more than four pieces.

25. Large pillows slightly worn with a slight yet distinctive odor from being thrown on the floor and serving as a dog bed.

26. Dog stairs to sofa, only necessary for the smallest of dogs; most dogs easily find their way onto the sofa without assistance.

27. Fridge photos revealing adorableness of your dog and a series of dog cartoons (All cartoons do seem to be made about your Adorable).

FRIDGE MAGNET ADVICE FOR ALL DOGS TO LIVE BY

If you are stumped about fridge bling the following can add to your home:

- Do what you dig and dig what you do.

- Chase what you fancy.

- Unleash your dreams.

- Never pass a lemonade stand without barking.

- Be loyal and faithful.

- Love unconditionally.

- Take joy rides, call shotgun, and stick your head out the window when you feel like it.

- Protect those you love.

- Mail delivery can be great if you make it fun.

- When loved ones come home, always run to greet them.

- Be a good listener.

THE FRIDGE OF

"Sam"

Sam gets very excited when the fridge is opened. Currently unable to open without human assistance.

AN ADORABLE

Two of the four shelves are dedicated to Adorable's food (and most of the freezer space).

- Don't hold grudges…be quick to forgive.

- You are not here to clean your own bottom.

- Play tirelessly and with abandon.

- Learn new tricks at any age.

- Anywhere you can reach with a lick is never out of bounds.

- Don't bite the hand that feeds you.

- Make new friends.

- A good run can make your day.

- Guests who don't greet and pet you first are the enemy.

- Respect authority.

- It's not the size of the dog in the fight, it's the size of the owner.

- Trust your instincts.

- Sniff out fun.

- Be brave.

- Remind all who'll listen that your nose is 50 times more powerful than a human's.

CHAPTER 8

FUR-SANITY: FINDING A SUPPORT SYSTEM FOR YOUR ADORABLE

The friends of furry Adorables know the secret to living life in an effortless, orderly fashion. Is it organization? Complete devotion to your Adorable? No, it's support systems!

Your dog's health, wellbeing, fame, coat sheen, and longevity are not made into reality by you but, in fact, by the numerous support staff around you that help you perfect a connection with your dog and the wider (online) world.

The dog lover prides herself on getting out and about with a well-turned-out pal and maintaining a hair-free, organized existence, but she needs assistance to get there. Dog families depend on auxiliary support, known as help, or if you're insensitive, "the help." The members of your support team may vary: an apartment-dweller will not need a gardener but hiring a housekeeper is a no-brainer. A complete list of support team options appears below.

Service providers are everywhere and show up in unique places. They are all spiritually linked to the cause of making your Adorable and his surroundings the best that they can be. Labor, loyalty, and technical expertise all contribute to adorableness and can even provide you with world event updates that you may have missed. It's bound to happen from time to time due to your discussion about the merits of raw versus commercial food at the dog park.

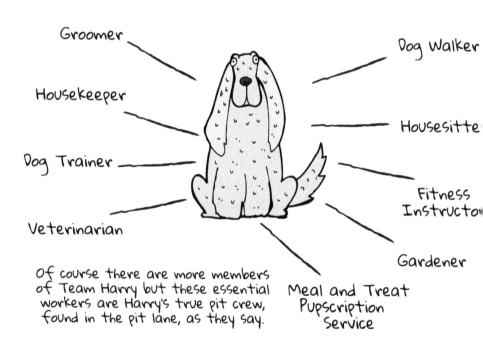

TEAM HARRY
Support Systems that Lead to an Adorable Existence

Groomer

Housekeeper

Dog Trainer

Veterinarian

Dog Walker

Housesitter

Fitness Instructor

Gardener

Of course there are more members of Team Harry but these essential workers are Harry's true pit crew, found in the pit lane, as they say.

Meal and Treat Pupscription Service

GROOMER

The leader of the support system.

Entrusted with the look of your pet and the wellbeing and health of his skin and nails. After an extensive discussion of products to be used on Harry and a tour of back-of-house to assess cleanliness, the leash is handed over and she operates solo.

She knows it's hard for you to be apart from Harry but patience and following instructions regarding when your pet's grooming session is complete are very important. It is preferable to hire a mobile groomer so that you are always in close proximity when work is being done and Harry does not have to be shuttled to the pet parlor in his pre-groomed state. Harry's groom time should be used as "you" time. If you don't take care of yourself how can you take care of your little star? Your happiness and confidence benefit your dog like a good body scrub does your clogged pores.

Your groomer is an artist. You just must watch the documentary *Well Groomed* to understand that most groomers take their craft very seriously. This is no two-week course and certificate prior to bearing down on unsuspecting pets with sharp clippers. The staff at Supercuts may take on their career in such a manner but not your pet groomer. Most are well-trained and dedicated to their profession. To keep a good one you need to treat them right.

WHAT NOT TO SAY TO YOUR GROOMER

- He is an angel, don't worry.

- I don't know why he has so many mats, but please keep the length.

- Are you sure that shampoo is organic?

- He periodically drags his

bottom along the grass for God-knows-what reason.

- Why did it take so long?

- It's too short. I told you to leave it long.

- He's a purebred poodle; do you know how to do proper poodle cuts?

- He has never had his nails done. Could you make sure you get to those?

- We just went to the beach.

- Can you do a mobile service without charging for travel time?

- Do you do any A-list celebrities' puppies?

- Are you the owner of this pet salon? I've heard that you do not need to tip the owner.

- Can I see your professional liability insurance?

- Why are you so slow?

DOG WALKER

Before choosing any dog walker, make sure that they describe their service as "amazing dog walker," "spiritual dog walker," or "athletic dog walker." It's best to stay away from combo services "walker/groomer," "walker/trainer," or "walker/shisperer." If they can't focus on their business model, they can't focus on walking your precious. This is important because they are entrusted with keys and have full access to your home. They are expected to take your Adorable for an enjoyable walk just as you would and play fetch for an extended period. Some may have other dogs to walk at the same time, which is acceptable so long as your Adorable gets ample solo attention.

If your Adorable has too much energy in the evening and you suspect he was shorted on his walk consider installing a remote camera to view comings and goings. You may also then need to navigate awkward discussions on the appropriate length of a walk and reasons why your cookie jar is always empty and your espresso machine dirty.

HOUSE SITTER

This invaluable partner arrives when you take those inevitable vacations and weekends out of town. Their stay may include being entrusted with your pet so it's critical to find a reliable and trusted soldier who feels comfortable enough in your home to interact as you would with your Adorable but not so comfortable as to have dinner parties, in clothes procured from your closet, after a bubble bath in your master bath clawfoot, all while ignoring your Adorable. During the first overnight stay, your pup should be fitted with a GoPro camera in his collar to track minute-by-minute coddling. Once trust is built up with your sitter, it will only be necessary to hide cameras in knickknacks in every room.

HOUSEKEEPER

One, two, or three times a week, the housekeeper changes bedding, sweeps under furniture, and removes hair from obvious and non-obvious places. They are an outsider, not accustomed to scents and grunge from your Adorable. But, to thoroughly remove the scent and grunge, a third-party independent is necessary. This team member sometimes forgets instructions, uses too much bleach, and washes your Adorable's dog bed with scented detergent procured in haste to remove dog dinge as opposed to the organic cleaners your beloved's skin is accustomed to. For their first visit a GoPro camera should be installed in your pup's collar.

DOG TRAINER

At times, no amount of YouTube or binge-watching Cesar Millan can produce all the answers as to why your dog refuses to come when called or will not stay off the furniture, or worse. Engaging a dog trainer, just as when you finally find the need to engage a personal trainer, will remove all excuses and ensure that "it" gets done, whatever "it" may be.

You may need them weekly, and they will most always leave homework. It will be well worth the investment to reign in your natural proclivity to be permissive, which may be taken advantage of by your Adorable. Said proclivity may require course-corrective action, preferably before it gets out of hand and requires the premium package, which costs four times more. Just note that for centuries, charges of Adorables have been taught never to hire a trainer who was born in any country beginning with the letter "G."

MEAL AND TREAT PUPSCRIPTION SERVICE

Arrives monthly to great anticipation by all in a nice box that's left by the door. Creatures that live in the wild will attack and devour the box within an hour of its arrival so you may need to rely on your neighbor to move it to a safe place or out of the sun. It's prudent to install a porch camera to ensure that such important packages are not commandeered by others that may want to try the delicious gems without pressing the "buy" button.

GARDENER

Unnecessary for city dwellers. Entrusted with mowing lawn and general cleanup. Services generally do not include removal of pet waste unless you pay extra, though certain gardener services have gotten wise and offer cleanup services along with landscaping. He will pick up your pup's natural fertilizer and wrap it in a plastic bag. Then he will open another, bigger plastic bag, pull out chemical fertilizer, and spread it around your yard.

This is why some clients don't warn of the yard presents and wait for the weedwhacker to spray dog waste throughout the yard. Unfortunately, this may land on him like confetti at a wedding and inevitably end up on his boots, equipment, and in his truck and will only lead to him cursing you and your Adorable. Your yard will be organically fertilized but be forewarned: such events will cause him to leave your employ despite adorable greetings from your Adorable and the odd treat bundle offering in the holidays.

VETERINARIAN

You will have a better relationship with your vet if you have procured pet insurance. However, her services are necessary either way. She brings an air of competence only before seen in your investment banker. Confidence that communicates that everything possible is being done for your dog.

Her diploma, certificates, and affiliations are all prominently displayed to justify the shocking charges. You walk away with a significantly lighter wallet each time even when simply arriving for a seemingly basic service such as an ear clean, but you know that she has done the best for your dog's benefit.

Good veterinary care is also measured by communication; a disarming call from your vet before you redial (again) to check up on your Adorable is dramatically satisfying, especially if the news is good. She can also be seen around town partak-

A CAUTIONARY TAIL:
Pet Insurance: Only for those Living on the Edge or for All?

A young woman, who had worked in veterinarian offices for over 20 years and was no stranger to their billing practices, greeted her daily life in the resigned fashion that at some point she would join the ranks with a vet bill so large she could have bought a new car or gone on an extended European vacation.

Despite this acceptance, all seemed fine with her pets most of the time. She quit saving to a special account specifically opened for future vet care. She reasoned that with all the offices she had worked in over the years she likely would get a significant discount when her time came.

That was until one morning when, jolting her roommates awake, she came running, half naked, from her bedroom holding her black Pug puppy with his eye hanging out. She needed assistance to hold him so she could get dressed and get to the vet— most likely not to save the eye but to spend several thousand unexpected dollars on her Pug's recovery and passage to a full-time, fun-filled life as a pirate, and on her own therapy to manage the trauma. (Note: this is what did occur.)

Like all insurance costs, the monthly fees for pet insurance are hard to swallow. If you do decide to go for it, Lemonade, Inc., claim to be transforming the very business model of insurance by creating an insurance experience that is fast, affordable, and hassle-free. One that the long-time veterinary care worker would have likely appreciated.

Despite the hefty cost of pet insurance premiums, a majority of those with Adorables have diverted their monthly payment to Spotify instead. They have rationally considered that if their Pug puppy's eyeball falls out it would not be covered by insurance just like their Aunt Sally's car incident with the biker, that demanded immediate payment for the arm hanging the incorrect way.

To save money, you can choose a higher deductible. If you video your little star going through procedures at the vet, you can usually set up a Go Fund Me page and pay for the whole procedure and a spa treatment for you.

ing in improv with the local stage group but that is not why her deep personal concern for the injury of your pet came across as similar to the loss of her own grandmother. In the end, you did your research, and you trust her with Harry's life. She deserves your faith in her— and acupuncture does not cure everything. With today's multiple cable channels and streaming services four out of every five vets have their own TV show; it's usually best to avoid those unless they guarantee a four-episode story arc for your pet.

FITNESS INSTRUCTOR

Acronyms are oft used and sometimes recognizable like JD, MD, PFT, and the like but lately, the owners of Adorables have had an eye out for CCFTs—Certified Canine Fitness Trainers. These specially trained people have a superior understanding of canine body mechanics, anatomy, functional movement, behavior, nutrition, and the fundamentals of canine fitness and conditioning. When Harry (and perhaps you) are thicker than desired around the middle one call will set you on a course-correcting path. You won't simply both take up frisbee golf or do that extra loop around the block; you'll do it with the correct form.

In the event the spa is not a viable option in your world there are other ways to get the essentials done. Here is one tactic to successfully achieve a home petticure.

HOW TO CUT YOUR DOGS NAILS

Most dogs do not like their nails being cut so various processes have been developed to manage this issue

1. Apply plastic wrap around head.

2. Apply peanut butter to plastic wrap.

3. Procure nail clippers.

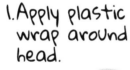

4. Allow dog to lick peanut butter, and while dog is distracted by deliciousness (and hopefully you are not) cut nails.

CHAPTER 9

LOVE THY NEIGHBOR: YOUR ADORABLE'S BIGGEST FAN SHOULD BE HER COMMUNITY

Neighbors are a fact of life, no matter in the city, suburbs, or most rural locations, although the proximity demanded by each may dictate the level of good behavior required. Neighbors can keep an eye out for your packages, provide a cup of sugar in the middle of a recipe, and may even turn into a friend and confidant. However, care must be taken as the social construct of the neighborhood is a delicate one and laden with opportunity for fandom; it's also where your biggest enemy may lie without you being able to hit the "block" button.

Never has the term, "Keep your friends close, and your enemies closer," been more important and more true.

No Adorable wants to step out of their home to be met with glaring and suspicious neighbors or give them fodder to post negative comments on the neighborhood chat room, or worse, social media. In such cases you may be compelled to respond in kind by commenting on their children, a car on blocks in their driveway, or late-night police visits to investigate screaming. The point isn't that these things happen—and if they're going to talk about your Adorable in that manner it's only fair you retaliate—but such behaviors are unnecessary and undermine confidence along with, more importantly, your Adorable's path to fandom.

Although neighborhood landmarks vary, there are some things Adorables can count on in a typical neighborhood. Here's how to navigate these landmarks to ensure you are making fans and not foes and that you only have to buy one carton of eggs for eating and not a second one for throwing.

Traditional Neighbor Definition

noun: *a person living in direct proximity to another.*

Definition of Neighbor for Adorables

noun: *a person or dog living on the daily walk route or that can hear a bark relative to the location of the dog referred to.*

The definition of a neighbor for Adorables is far more expansive than for humans and therefore encompasses more people, who must be taken into consideration.

MAKING FANS FOR YOUR ADORABLE

Kids. Some say that the quickest way to a parent's heart is through kindness to their children. That means that rather than cowering at a hand flying at his face without warning for an awkward pat, your Adorable should instead look pleased to have the attention and "lean in," as the Silicon Valley crowd say. For those children without a family pet, your Adorable can be their muse, gaining a loyal fanbase that will grow for years to come. You, in turn, could attract an appreciative (and free) dog walker who beams at the thought of saying to passers-by, "He's not my dog, but he loves me and I love him." Parents in tow of such children will appreciate the extra two minutes of solace resulting from your Adorable's reliable babysitting. #newfamilyfans

Lawn Love and Respect. You will, at least once, have seen a sign in your neighborhood stuck into very green and perfectly mowed grass and placed there, oftentimes, by a current or former board member of the homeowners' association with the words "My Yard is Not Your Dog's Toilet." This is worth respecting even if you always had the intention of picking up your dog's waste and knew in your heart that the quality food you provide your Adorable would make an excellent fertilizer for this dedicated landscaper.

For some, lawns represent success: a true physical manifestation of the American Dream of homeownership; a reflection that they care about belonging and want others to note their fastidious nature. You thought he was simply an obsessive dictator but now that you know different you must respect his wishes. So, you can *think* the A-word, you just can't say it.

EVERY ADORABLE DESERVES STAR TREATMENT. GET EXCLUSIVE CONTENT AT THEPOPULARPETS.COM

TYPICAL SIGN SIGHTING OF A DEDICATED LANDSCAPER
(REPORTEDLY FOUND IN EVERY SUBURBAN NEIGHBORHOOD IN THE US)

Other Dogs Are Allies. Odds are there will be another Adorable in the street, barking from behind a fence, at the park, or on a walk. Although annoying, these are your allies. These Adorables and their charges are the ones with the highest likelihood of backing you up in a scuffle—the storyline found in all great telenovelas and Hallmark Channel movies since there is no story without a great back-up character (or an unwanted pregnancy).

As annoying as it may be to listen to a dog barking through the fence as you also listen to his "parent," as she refers to herself, tell you all about his many attributes, these same passionate "parents" will have your back if the homeowners' association or a disgruntled party in the neighborhood comes down on you.

Cars Can Only Be Pee'd on in Complete Secrecy. Car tires, for some reason, rank high in a dog's hierarchy of places to pee on. Covered with scents from the road, and other dogs, they beckon to your furry friend to press the "reply" button and send a pee-mail. This calling card is a way to get a message to other dogs that follow him to the tire.

Car owners generally do not like pee-stained tires and rims. There is also a direct correlation between the shinier rims and how angrily the vehicle owner will respond to pee on his tires. This proves that dogs have a sense

Vertical Objects that Serve as an Alternative to Car Tires

Horizontal Objects that do NOT Serve as an Alternative to Car Tires

of humor.

When you take your Adorable out for his walks, let him leave his calling card on vertical surfaces, such as hydrants, mailboxes, or the elderly. This will make it easier for his pals to pick up the message. There are a ton of other vertical options that don't involve using the neighbors' vehicles (unless no one's around).

On another note, your little buddy will get a bad reputation if he jumps up on a visitor's car. He will cause damage to your sister-in-law's new Tesla, which can lead to scratches on both the door and her psyche.

Ignore Bikes. Loud children love competing for the sidewalk with their bikes. Large neighbors in tight spandex will appear regularly on the road. Your Adorable should be trained to ignore both and you should be trained to get him out of the way. Many accidents occur from cyclists trying to avoid Adorables that mean well. Keep your Adorable out of their direct path. This will prevent you being in the unenviable position of having to awkwardly stand over an injured cyclist with dog in tow that is trying to lick injured party's face and having to bake cookies to wish them a speedy recovery. If the cyclist is unconscious, licking is okay as a revival method.

Avoid Elderly Angst. The elderly are the central repository of all goings on in the neighborhood. They are always watching and listening. Depending on age they may be stationed at a window or out in a front yard. Your Adorable's image must be kept pristine since ultimately any misdoings will be spread throughout the neighborhood faster than a double viral post. Of course, due to hearing issues often the gossip of, "Your dog knocked over a child," will become, "Mary met a crocodile," so, this isn't a major worry, but if an elderly neighbor shows any interest in your Adorable, provide some treats for her to give him.

From that day forward, he will greet her with a hopeful look and an adorable face in anticipation of treats. She will thereafter believe this look is a desire for her company, which bodes very well since she loves attention as much as your Adorable. For a final bonding trick, every time she asks how old your pup is, always respond that it's her exact age in dog years but you wonder why she appears more spry than him.

Parks Can Make or Break You. If there is one in your neighborhood, it's the center of the action. Parents sit on benches in rows facing their children and discuss their attributes and personality traits. If it's a dog park, substitute dogs for children and the story remains the same. Since at each the focus is on the charges, your Adorable's behavior will also fall under scrutiny if he does anything other than lie under a tree. Socialization occurs at a young age and will ensure that your Adorable can get along with other dogs and children. Demonstrate that he is gentle and that you are capable of corrective action if you hear whispering from the sidelines. Action on your part to enforce good behavior will be appreciated and solidify your Adorable's reputation as a lovely neighborhood dog from a respectable family. On the flip side, if your neighbors are all horrible—they play loud music late, throw cigarette butts in your yard, and don't take care of theirs—there are numerous dogs you can adopt to your loving home that, when let free in a park, can terrorize with just their menacing grin and speedy approach, thus invoking that may just invoke improved behavior.

Strategies for Handling the Dog-Hater Neighbor. Sometimes an extremely adorable dog, apologies, cookies, and a commitment to prohibit barking in the future is simply not enough. The hatred could have been born from a small transgression by you or Harry or be so deeply ingrained from dog-hater parents that your neighbor's dislike for all things dog cannot be overcome on your watch, only in front of a trained psychotherapist. This is fine but neighborly harmony is important so here are a few tips to turn that relationship around.

1. Respect their wishes. If not traipsing on their lawn is a directive written on a small sign, even though said sign is placed in a common area, just follow orders.

2. Smile. Killing with kindness is century-old rhetoric for a reason. Grumbling within earshot about how kooky they are, although tempting, is passive aggressive and unhelpful.

3. Find common ground. Detect an interest in drones? Learn about drones and drop a factoid or an inquiry about their interest on your next cruise by and talk about how you love the excitement of that whirring sound and this riveting pastime. It may be helpful to note that your brother-in-law also has this hobby and maybe they should meet on his next visit.

What to Do and Not to Do If the Police Are Called

Living in close proximity to people you have nothing in common with, aside from a similar commute, can become charged. You would hope that a discussion or at least a note would be left for you before police show up to mediate a dispute amongst neighbors but alas, sometimes the authorities are called to intervene.

Despite being placed in the hot seat and the embarrassing lights:

Do

- Stay calm,

- Be apologetic for their time being wasted,

- - Be clear about your side, the correct side,

- Have a well-behaved Harry at your side to show how lovely he is, and,

- Mention just enough denigrating things about the tattletale that are not relevant to the issue so that they see he is the offender, and that you and Harry are the sane, good actors in this scene. Some phrases to add include, "He seems particularly anxious all the time, I'm concerned about his mental state." "He has been out of town a lot lately—I heard it was for inpatient treatment. Perhaps he is stressed as a result of his experience."

Then drop a couple of $20 bills out of your pocket, thank them, and walk inside.

Don't

- Apologize to the officer that this small dispute took him away from his donuts,

- Argue with the officer regarding the facts of the matter in dispute,

- Discuss the weapons that you have available in storage if this behavior continues,

- Aggressively indicate that your dog is the best and has never done anything wrong, and,

- Be snarky and say, "Wow, big man. Don't you have some real crimes to solve down at 5.0 HQ?"

Then drop a couple of $20 bills out of your pocket, thank them, and walk inside.

A TRUE CAUTIONARY TAIL: "GOOD FENCES MAKE GOOD NEIGHBORS" IS NOT HOLLOW RHETORIC

A young man inherited a house in Bellevue, Washington, at the age when parties took priority over house maintenance, consideration of neighbors was not forefront of the mind, and a home was merely thought of as a house. After being denied a childhood pet his entire life, he jumped at this newfound opportunity to exert his freedom and get a dog. He appeared to attempt to make up for lost time in size and cuteness by selecting an incredible looking blue Neapolitan mastiff, the type that weighs more than you do when fully grown, requires steady training, and dislikes being alone. Originally, the dog was a priority, but before long priorities shifted, and the dog was just left in the yard to amuse itself. It was formerly a grassy backyard but was now a mud pit.

Upon arrival home one day instead of a nose and paws peeking over a fence, the young man was met in the driveway by the son of the commanding next-door neighbor, a meek 15-year-old boy, who was generally nervous either due to genetics or as a learned behavior due to the overbearing nature of his parents. On this day, the general fearfulness he seemed to typically possess appeared amplified as he was waiting wide-eyed and panicked.

He explained that the dog had broken out of the yard and into his, and after ransacking the yard had broken into his house.

It was time to inspect the mass destruction. The young dog owner yearned for days past when he would be sent over to the neighbors' house by his dad to apologize for a simple noise complaint.

When they got to the site of the massacre, they found stark similarities to a house party the dog owner once attended in high school that had got out of hand—described by many as reminiscent of what a pack of bikers leaves behind after a riot. Outside, lawn furniture knocked over and eaten; inside, couch cushions mauled; books off shelves; remote controls covered with chew marks; the large television and artwork crooked and falling off the walls. Astonishingly, he later recalled looking at the wall and ceiling to see large, muddy pawprints. Oh, and there was a distinct and incredible pungent wet-dog odor that filled the air of this formerly dog-free home.

Many thoughts ran through his head: fear of retribution, cost of repair... how athletic and focused his dog was to do this damage. He wondered why he had not taken his neighbor up on the offer to share the cost of a new fence. These thoughts all occurred while he stood, mouth agape, taking in this amazing sight, every so often blurting out an inappropriate laugh.

Despite efforts to remedy the situation and replace certain items, neighborly relations were never repaired and Baker, as was his name, never became the iconic Adorable of the neighborhood that his looks had set him up for. Dogs need exercise and attention; they will find a way to get it, and sometimes in a destructive way. Good fences make good neighbors, but more importantly, so do giant dogs that get exercised.

MATCH THE NEIGHBOR
WITH THE BEHAVIOR

Puts a sign in yard that reads, "Do not let your dog poop in our yard."

Tom, a veteran with two kids, who works from home.

Texts you constantly, swearing your dog was in their yard.

Susie, a retired schoolteacher with a new Lhasa apso.

Bends down and gives your dog a love every time you pass.

Jean, a busy professional with two kids and two labs, who seems to be running 100 miles an hour.

Donna, a retired fish and game worker, who still volunteers on weekends at the local park showing kids different types of wild animal manure.

Offers to walk your dog when you are at work.

Dan, retired accountant, who now spends his working hours on lawn maintenance, which his wife appreciates.

Suggests that you may want to put your dog on a raw diet.

Dear Kendra,

My neighbor swears that my dog is more into him than me. That is just ridiculous, after all I have been by Fudge's side through thick and thin. I buy him expensive dog food and treats, I pay for Stan to come walk him, I take him to the groomer and to the vet when he is sick whereas all my neighbor does is pass him a treat and play with him at the dog park now and again. How can I confirm whether or not Fudge likes my neighbor better?

Thank you,
Seeking Confirmation of Love

....

Dear Seeking Confirmation of Love,

First, it is likely that Fudge does like your neighbor more than you. All the things you mention you do for Fudge are paid for by you but are not "done" by you. Granted, you are not a vet, but do you ever give Fudge attention like your neighbor does? Here are some handy little questions to confirm the way of Fudge's true heart:

1) When you're walking Fudge does he appear to recognize your neighbor's steps and turn around when he sees him?

2) Does Fudge elect to pee on all the other yards but not your neighbor's?

3) Does Fudge appear to talk about your neighbor to all his friends?

4) Does Fudge make eyes at your neighbor from across the dog park/street/local pet store?

5) Does Fudge pull on his leash on his walk so that you end up passing your neighbor's work just to say hi?

6) Does Fudge text or DM your neighbor back in a reasonable amount of time?

If you answer yes to more than two of the above, then you

have problem and you are going to have to up your game. Dogs' intuition is far superior to any human's and they don't play coy communication games. If he senses that you are not that into him, he will find love elsewhere, which it sounds like he already has. Sorry, Seeking Confirmation of Love, we cannot confirm love here.

—Kendra

THE HOMEOWNERS' ASSOCIATION (HOA)

Other than the board members of the HOA, it is rare to hear someone say, "I love my HOA." Comparable to the hall monitor that you mercilessly tortured in high school, the HOA has the obligation to legislate and enforce the rules referred to as CC&Rs (Declaration of Covenants, Conditions, and Restrictions) and instill order in the neighborhood with the long-term dual goal of maintaining property values and curbing the riffraff. Even if such riffraff is a paying homeowner.

It was once thought that the role of HOAs was to just mandate the approved colors of the structures, dictate appropriate holiday decorations, and get kickbacks from the landscape company they selected. But a far more important role is to field complaints from homeowners, which are usually made against the charges of Adorables.

DUTIES OF THE HOA IN A TYPICAL NEIGHBORHOOD

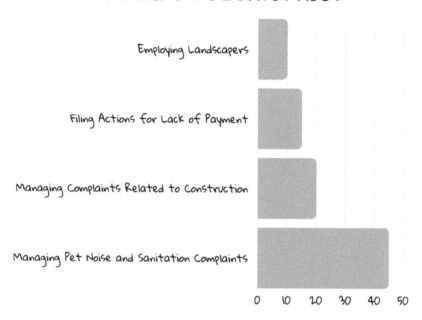

Once the HOA knows you by name life can become difficult. Even if they are wonderful people, the unbridled authority of being on the HOA can birth a power-crazed megalomaniac. Don't be the source of the most common complaints and be sure to note building restrictions and approval requirements if you want to build Harry that two-story palace. Defending your structure to these legislators and enforcers post construction is an uphill battle. Harry could suffer the brunt of your thoughtless decision-making, which he should not. It's far more savvy to become a board member yourself and use your power ethically and completely to benefit yourself.

CHAPTER 10

ADORABLE CHARACTER BUILDING FOR IRRESISTIBILITY

The Adorable's character is a hybrid of established petiquette, good behavior, and complete socialization weaved throughout his personality to build upon an already irresistible good nature. The charge of an Adorable ensures these are assimilated into life eventually, as if by osmosis. Deep down, the Adorable is ready to bust out a show tune if she could sing, play Twister if she could twist, and pour drinks for everyone from the keg if she had thumbs. At the same time, she's under complete control and will only get in the mix when appropriate. Fear and worry are not in her vocabulary—if she had a vocabulary.

Components of Character Development

Note some Adorables will have the components innately, whereas some may need your assistance, despite what a breeder tells you. You will play a role in shaping your Adorable.

WELL-SOCIALIZED

Your Adorable struts with confidence, hears a noise and does not fear it, hears kids playing in the park and looks on with curiosity as opposed to dread; she is excited, but not too excited, to greet other Adorables; she has been there done that and is as comfortable and natural in her world as Snoopy is sitting on his doghouse. She has a well-developed character as a result and is a well-socialized dog, used to different situations, which she embraces with enthusiasm and not foreboding. She is set up for success!

Like settling into any new work environment, it will take time for your Adorable to familiarize herself with new experiences and get used to being around different people and places. She's in control and evaluates when it's the right time to unleash her personality.

She's not that different from you. It took you several weeks to understand to stay away from Uncle Frank after Mondays, his apparent shower day. It

The Well Socialized Adorable

Smells like the ocean-Let's Go!

Is that my BFF barking? Let's Go!

Hey Kids - pet me!

Is that a parade? - Let's Go!

I love cars! Roll this window down and get moving! Let's Go!

The Unsocialized Adorable will replace the words "Let's Go" with "let's go home- that is scary."

took you a while to understand Sylvia, the office manager and the sips of her Friday libations that she kept hidden in her desk drawer in preparation for the weekend. It took you even longer to realize that Sylvia started this on Monday to recover from the weekend, and that Monday was her shower day, too.

Outings that familiarize your Adorable with many kinds of people, animals, and different sounds through various experiences are important. Treats will make experiences positive if they are not initially so. As a result, your Adorable will settle in, make sound judgments, and be a pleasure to be with. The following outings will assist with accomplishing those goals.

Play dates. So she can get to know a friend and learn how to play—not too aggressive, not too timid. Confidence will bloom so that when introduced to large groups she will not be overwhelmed but instead will lead the pack on a chase around the park. If little Sammy then takes charge at the dog park and finds creative ways to show dominance, you can apologize profusely for her assertiveness but deep down you know she will be the leader you've always raised. #girlboss

Dog Parks. Excellent opportunity for socialization and critical to networking and building a following, also to mingle and get referrals for dog-friendly restaurants, the latest tips on how to get "support dog status," and generally how you never have to leave your Adorable at home. Also continues to build confidence and the place where dogs really develop the unwritten rules of doggie communication not yet learned from their mother and siblings before being found by you or shipped to you. If it's possible to teach your Adorable any kind of trick in advance, this will set your little genius up for success. Kind of like doing your children's homework so they make friends with the right crowd. (Note: paying people to say they are on a water polo team to get into college is clearly going too far and can result in jail and bad publicity.) #knowyourlimits

Dog Beach. All the features of dog parks but also an education in sand, water, waves, and delectable picnics that should be ignored. Certain dogs will have a natural affinity for water while others may just enjoy the sand and digging holes. The only warning is to train your special one to avoid the large drooling dogs that abscond with her floaty without a human course correcting the bad behavior. #strangerdanger

Dining Out. Hopefully, a trip to a restaurant can occur after comportment at one of the other venues is mastered. Dining out is excellent practice for looking cute, being patient, sitting quietly, and drinking with poise. With such good manners, a dropped fork and delicious smells will leave your Adorable unfazed. The highest praise will be given by passers-by who didn't even realize you had brought your dog and they will loudly rave about your skills. This is also a great time to loudly call out your Instagram account name with the phrase, "I usually don't give out this information, but you can see her do tricks and wear cool outfits @...." #everymomentcounts

TRUE TAIL
Service Dog Sully: Proof of Ultimate Character

Service dogs are the ultimate well-socialized Adorables. Service companions must be able to handle a wide range of people and animals and are conditioned to properly react—or not react—to extra cuddles from passerby, smells, sounds, and even certain objects.

As President George Bush, Sr., aged, he needed help and, as a dog lover, it made sense to turn to the assistance of a dog. Sully provided emotional support and was trained to support President Bush with routine tasks. He learned to call for assistance when his charge required it, to open and close doors, and even oversee Operation Desert Storm, going on to provide advice to later Presidents. A support dog is an amazing testament to the capabilities of all dogs: they are apolitical and just want to make life better, but they are also utterly trainable, reliable, strategic, and sage.

GOOD PETIQUETTE

This second component of character is sometimes mistaken as mere politeness, as if looking cute and not barking at the neighbor is all that distinguishes an Adorable. On the contrary, petiquette is the Adorable's suit of armor and good petiquette has been reported to be strongly linked to a solid, well-developed character. When mishaps occur, as they will, good petiquette will ensure that there is no chink in the upstanding reputation of your Adorable and making the right choice subsequent to a mishap reflects on his well-established character.

QUIZ

The following quiz is designed to clarify some fine points of living with an Adorable with exemplary character—to spotlight decisions in four situations that only the charge of an Adorable with good petiquette would make. For those to whom good character and good sense is not obvious, the answers appear at the bottom of the page.

1 Your Adorable ran through your host's garden and peed on the pumpkins. You leave for home and...

A. Vehemently deny that your pup visited the back yard during the stay when asked if he got into the garden.

B. Call a few days later and discuss an article you read about the need to wash pumpkins prior to carving.

C. Mention that you know a great gardener and you are so thankful for your host's hospitality that you asked that he go over and make any repairs to the yard and correct any damage that your Adorable may have caused since you had to leave in such a rush.

D. Blame it on teenagers in the neighborhood.

2 At your neighborhood dog park, you notice someone did not clean up after their pet. You...

A. Ask loudly if the person did not see the bags at the entrance to the park.

B. Ignore the ignorance and rudeness and continue talking to Molly from your pet group about the benefits of a raw diet.

C. Go and pick up the waste yourself.

D. Call a local high school and complain to the principal that local teenagers have been leaving poop. This will usually cause a field trip organized by the angered principal to clean all dog parks within a five-mile radius of the school.

You are at a state park and there are signs everywhere about safe-guarding wildlife by keeping pets on a leash, but you are the only one for miles and you have never seen wildlife. You...

A. Let Buster off his leash, keep a watchful eye out for the ranger, and ponder the good old days when there were no rules.

B. Keep Buster on his leash until you get to the back country and then let him off, then write a blog on ridiculous park rules related to dogs and discriminatory behavior of old white men in power, particularly those that lead the Parks Service and make the rules.

C. Keep Buster on his leash but later write a letter to the Parks Service and ask about the sensitive animals and if there can be a designated trail that is off leash.

D. Let Buster off his leash and complain to the others at the park and later, in a sternly worded email to the Parks Service, about teenagers playing loud music and propose that they be on leashes.

You invite your friends and their Adorables over for lunch. One of your Adorable guests barfs on your rug. You...

A. Make the biggest deal possible so that they will buy you a new one.

B. Declare that your Adorable has never made messes like that, pass them the Miracle Spot Remover, and leave them to tend to lunch, which you declare no one likely has an appetite for now.

C. Tell the guest not to feel bad, it's an old rug. Remove it and call the cleaner. Express concern for the wellbeing of the offending Adorable.

D. Make a big deal about it and press that their teenager should clean your rug and entire house for that matter. Also, to seal the deal, mention that you've heard about what the teenagers have been doing at the dog park.

How did you do? In each case the answer is (c). Note that petiquette and a well-developed character are not confined to Adorables. As their charges, we need to make up for any deficiencies they have with sound character that will be imbued on them. The (d) answers are more fun if you're in the mood and subconsciously angry at a teenager but note that they are not reflective of good character.

SIGNS YOUR ADORABLE MAY HAVE BEEN NAUGHTY

A fresh pile of dirt close by

Tongue out and very thirsty (not because you took him for a run)

More dirt on paws than usual

Wet (not because of a bath)

A happy, self-satisfied look followed by exhaustion

An awful smell emanating from him that you do not recognize

Something unidentifiable stuck in his coat

A ripped-up toy in his bed that you may have not seen before

NOTE: physical indications (direct from your Adorable) that he may have been naughty, 77.2% of the time other people will simply tell you later about your Adorable's naughtiness. Caution: they may be angry.

GOOD BEHAVIOR

The good behavior component of your Adorable's character is something to be acquired like a new rawhide; any dog can sit or walk on a leash but an Adorable behaves in just the right way so that he is welcome at parties and on vacations. Your furry friend doesn't really mean to be naughty. Adult dogs and puppies alike who lack any direction or obedience training can find themselves literally in the doghouse.

Like, an overly grumpy neighbor, naughty behavior may arise for a variety of reasons, from attention-seeking to lack of direction and training, or it may simply be a phase in life. (Don't rule out a genetic defect, but don't rush to judgment either.) With basic obedience rules, positive socialization, and understanding your delinquent pooch may eventually start to behave better.

The charges of Adorables tend to love their pets so, and sometimes don't immediately recognize when naughty behavior has occurred. Here are some indications of naughty behavior.

Additional signs your Adorable has been naughty (less common but similarly indicative of naughtiness):

- He won't look at you when you call his name.

- It's quiet—too quiet.

- He randomly starts doing tricks that you didn't ask for.

- He pretends to be napping.

- He walks past with his head dragging on the floor.

- You smell barbecue sauce.

- He's got a donut box container on his head.

- You find used needles buried in the yard.

- A trail of blood or polyester filling leading to a crime scene.

If, in the moment, you need to change up "Adorable" with another phrase, here are some thoughts.

TOP ALTERNATIVE EXPRESSIONS FOR NAUGHTY DOGS

- The Happy Hooligan

- The Mistake Missile

- Bad to the Bone

- Rebellious Rufus

- Disorderly Dan

- Seeker of Fun

- Bad Apple

- Wayward

- Monkey

- Mischievous

- Scheming Mimi

- Defiant

- Unruly

- Good Time Georgie

- Accident Waiting to Happen

- Your Troubled Teen

- Joey the Knife

- Puppy Mill Pete

- On the Way to a Dirt Nap

- Ready for a Big Dog Spanking

CHAPTER 11

THE DOG SHOW WORLD AND YOU

ORIGINS OF DOG SHOWING

Many years ago, before follower counts on Instagram and highly developed breed characteristics there was no way to measure the myriad aspects of the dog. So much so, that most dogs weren't even given names other than Dog, Mutt or…Dog. Dogs wandered about, nameless, being dogs, with a shared love of outdoors and companionship and dedication to their charges. Dogs were dogs and although they had skills, their charges were unable to distinguish who had the most athletic, best conformation, retrieved the fastest, and had the most fans.

Then in 1859, one of the first exhibitions took place in Newcastle-up-on-Tyne, with 50 entries—23 pointers and 27 setters. This was a step in the right direction, but there were still bugs to be worked out. There were three judges: it is said that a judge for the setters took first prize in the

THE GREAT

Our Furry Friends' Path to Judgment

Dogs Domesticated from wolves

First Dog Show created to measure dog

AKC judges' standards born ensuring that pug without a flat face would not win

Proliferation of dog breeders resulting in faster than normal progression of dogs that meet breed standards

20,000–40,000 BCE*

Dog first contributes to betterment of life through protection, hunting, tracking, and pulling sleighs

Dogs frustrated with having to make up for humans' failings – Aggressive Incident Arise with Bad Outcomes

Lassie was born and the first commercial dog food developed. Pets now allowed inside homes and quickly on beds

*There is some dispute about this actual date but we do know it was before the first dog show

pointer group, while a judge for the pointers took first prize in the setters group, which threw the entire exhibition into question. In awe, the sign-up form for judges went up 1,000% and to this day here has never been a shortage of judges available to judge our four legged friends.

Further attempts were made in Chelsea in 1863 with the Grand National Exhibition of Sporting and Other Dogs, which had 1,214 entries and 15 judges and in 1874 when the Illinois State Sportsman Association in Chicago put on the first show in the United States. However, without the American Kennel Club, there was no order, rules, or breed standards to follow. Instead, the judges were asked to write a critique about each dog, which even back then would not have included bow-legged and cross-eyed.

TIMELINE

Internet was born and progressed from file sharing to information transmission

First pug won Westminster with flattest face ever seen on any pet

Petco proliferated into 140 stores with online presence. Pet luxuries were available to the masses and shopping with your pet arrived in America

"Best in Show," the Dog Show mockumentary opened millions more eyes to the world of dog shows

2002

Disgruntled spouse frustrated with dog receiving more attention. Aggressive Incidents Arise at dog shows with Bad Outcomes

Westminster Dog Show first televised

Dogs frustrated with deformities resulting from breed characteristics – Aggressive Incidents arise with Bad Outcomes for show attendees

Handbag dogs were born and first appeared on fashion runways

National Dog Show aired after Macy's Thanksgiving Parade. 18 M people tuned in

Every dog got an award for participation as most young children do today.

Due to the lack of standards, it was not long before judges were confused and people began saying ,"My dog's better than your dog," while the inevitable response of, "Okay, show me," was met with a quizzical look. They began to wonder, "What standard am I aspiring to?" And, "How can I devote my life to my dog's superiority if there is no consistent goal?" Remember, there were no streaming services back then and citizens were mostly trying to find a reason for living.

It was clear that some structure was necessary in the form of consistent dog shows that culminated in an award and recognition. So, when some-

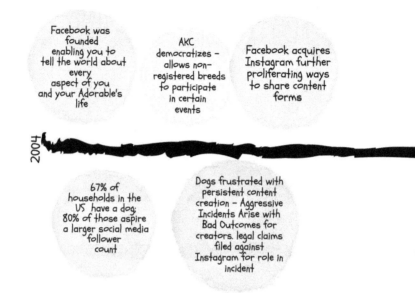

one claimed, "My dog is the champion," everyone knew categorically how excellent they really were, and that it was not simply because they were having a good hair day or a judge.

The show that fit this order was the Westminster Dog Show.

In 1907, a gentleman from the Westminster Kennel Club sought to find third-party support for claims to have the best dog, which at the time was primarily pointers and setters. The first Madison Square Garden show was born, produced by the Westminster Kennel Club. It has answered the question of which dog is best for the longest time as it is the longest continuous sporting event in America, except for the Kentucky Derby. Coincidentally, large hats and mint juleps appear at both events.

Since 1907, a dog has been able to win Best in Show at Westminster despite power shortages, storms, national depressions, World Wars, and global pandemics. Most dog owners admire the title but know their Adorable

@DougthePug won People's Choice award spurred by his giant social media following (in the millions)

Dog accounts on social media outrank people accounts by 2:1

Covid-19 spurs the largest growth in pet procurement ever in history and fostering social media fame harder than ever as dog shows cancelled

2020

Huge proliferation of dog sports; dog ice Hockey event draws millions of viewers to previously abandoned cable channels

Dock diving becomes more popular than football resulting in Aggressive Incidents due to proliferation of water borne ear infections in dogs

Amazing dog book comes on market which attempts to make sense of it all and leads to improved quality of content and proliferates sharing and content creation

is truly the best dog. To them, Westminster is just a curiosity, like Ripley's Believe It or Not! Most often the answer is "not."

The path to dog show champion does not begin with Westminster, however, and is not for the faint of heart. Before dogs are judged by American Kennel Club representatives, they must earn blue ribbons as they progress through the multitude of other qualifying shows and rounds. Blue ribbons and a spendthrift handler are your Adorable's only ticket to the Westminster Dog Show (even if you are a judge) in the first instance and the chance of winning Best in Show.

At the inception of Westminster an entire industry and commercial ecosystem was birthed that involved breeders, luxury goods, handlers, professional judges, sponsors, sex workers and media. Within a few years, no one would question the motivation to cultivate a breed for purely aesthetic satisfaction fueled by detailed breed standards.

Dachshund Breed Characteristics (just the hindquarters)

Breed Standards

Like natural predation, canine breed classification has been around for centuries, the first attempt being found in *A Treatise on Englische Dogges* by Dr. Johannes Caius, published in 1576, where he divides the many different breeds into three grand classifications: Sporting Dogs, Useful Dogs Otherwise Employed, and Toys. For years, sporting dog fans complained about the word "useful" not being applied to them, but they were never able to make a good enough case to switch.

These strict classifications and segregation would be for naught, however, without breed standards. To be a judge one must thoroughly know the breed standards of the judged. Breed standards, many of which date back to the Victorian era, are remarkably detailed. Take for instance the dachshund:

Long croup full, robustly muscled. and only slightly sloping toward tail (similar to an actual hot dog at angle of entry in mouth)

Pelvis strong, set obliquely – not too short

Rump full, broad and strong (similar to many notable Influencers)

Upper thigh set at right angles to pelvis, strong and of good length

Lower thigh short set at right angles to upper thigh and well muscled

Legs when seen from behind set well apart, straight and parallel, hind dewclaws undesirable

Pliant muscles (exact definitions of swimsuit models of the era)

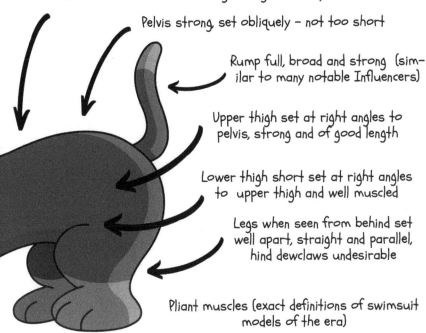

And that's just the hindquarters. There are also detailed specifications for general appearance, characteristics ("intelligent, lively, courageous to the point of rashness"), temperament ("faithful, versatile, good-tempered"), head and skull, eyes ("almond-shaped"), ears ("mobile"), mouth, neck, forequarters, body, feet, tail, gait, coat, color ("no white permissible, save for a small patch on chest, which is permitted but not desirable"), and, controversially, size—between 9 kg and 12 kg (controversial, because there are suggestions that some owners starve their dachshunds ahead of shows to ensure that they make their fighting weight). In the late 1800s there was literally nothing to do and that's why these rules exist.

Janet Jones
and Her
Children

Beth Strand
and Boots

Eddie Segal

DOG SHOW PLAYERS

MRS. KATHERINE KINGSLEY, OWNER & DOG SHOW ELITE

Mrs. Katherine Kingsley, third generation dog show participant and owner of Miss Abelee Scrocum Trodder, a King Charles spaniel from the great descendant lines of the bitch Mrs. Abelee Stranton Crest and the sire Mr. Abelee Scrocum Trodder (the bitch's brother). Recognizes that inbreeding like this in other species was responsible for a third nipple and is only seen in bluebloods and the smallest Appalachian towns but nevertheless Miss Abelee has mercilessly progressed through the dog show world with steam. Each day Mrs. Kingsley closes with a gratitude practice recommended by her niece and a recently televised, "Eye on Health" segment: "I am so grateful that Miss Abelee can maintain her pristine show record and is not cross-eyed."

MR. MARKS, PROFESSIONAL HANDLER

Owns kennel, an assortment of tuxedos, and 15 Afghan hounds that live indoors. Has been showing dogs since he was 15 years old. Tells the same story at each prospective client meeting about the extreme joy and satisfaction he had with the sport and the expert judging that had him win Best in Breed at Westminster with his beloved Bridget in 1982. Knows names of each breed winner since the inception of Westminster but does not know the names of his nieces or nephews.

MS. BAGLEY, AKC CERTIFIED JUDGE

A walking reference book of breed knowledge. An odd confidence seen only in a Chihuahua in heat amongst mastiffs Ms. Bagley is revered by the dog show community not because they recognize the power she wields over their lives with a mere gesture in their direction with her index finger but rather for her vast knowledge of everything dog and her willingness to share. (That is if you come to her farm with a checkbook and buy one of her prized champion's offspring.) Has judged Best in Show more times than any other judge. Wears her great authority in the dog show community as comfortably as her yearly purchase of her sensible tweed skirt suit from Talbots.

JANET JONES AND HER CHILDREN

Travelled from Akron, Ohio, for their 15th annual family visit to Westminster. The Westminster tradition started as a result of Janet's fond memories as a child of going to Westminster with her own parents before the dawn of the iPad and sitting in the audience for four days straight with a bruised rear. A sunny disposition caused her to gain an interest in the dog show world as opposed to sitting in despair for the duration. The annual family trips to Westminster now bring more excitement than a prospective trip to Disneyland (at least for Janet). Her kids now get to relive her childhood and listen to her riveting dog show tales. Janet can repeat statistics for all dogs and has secretly placed a 1:10 bet on wirehaired terriers being the breed of Best in Show. As of this writing Best in Show is the only bet Vegas is taking on Westminster, otherwise Janet would have made a handler bet and put $1,000 for her favorite handler (who she stalks on social media when the kids are at school) to win.

BETH STRAND, HANDLER/OWNER/AGILITY CHAMPION

Former high school field hockey champion turned dog agility trainer and handler of Boots Special Edge, a bright, anxious border collie agility pro that can read hand signs faster than the most renowned pitchers can read signals from their catchers Runs dog agility training school in a freezing/sweltering metal barn on their farm specifically built for Beth and her dogs.

Married to an accountant, who supports the aspirations of his wife to have a Westminster agility champion. Husband commutes an hour and fifteen minutes to work and back and gets up to feed on Sundays so that Beth can have her rural property and run her "dog business" that he has not seen make a profit from since its inception—he is, after all, the authority on profit and loss. Nevertheless, he is a dedicated dog show supporter, dutifully at ringside with water, extra treats, and towels, willing the pair to stardom while simultaneously providing statistical analysis of times and obstacles with his keen understanding of how it affects overall score, win record, and his strained financial existence.

EDDIE SEGAL, DEGENERATE GAMBLER
(not present at Westminster but instead views the show from the corner of a dingy Las Vegas sports bar)

Eddie is one of a group of tortured souls who cannot pass up an opportunity to wager on a televised contest of uncertain outcome. Is not turned off by the daunting task of picking a Westminster breed winner even with the expected featuring of 2,000 dogs representing 185 breeds in seven groups. His keen grasp of odds allows him to understand that breed eligibility grew by 16 percent over the last 10 years. A mixture of desperation and intelligence provides an awareness of dog types of which the common individual has never heard along with their specific notable bloodlines. Watches his liquid intake as he prefers to not go to the bathroom too often during the index finger wag—the most important part. Recognizes that picking a winner with the many variables of dog showing is a humbling undertaking that he does not undertake lightly.

He has spent months drafting a pro/con list, running hundreds of Monte Carlo simulations; he even consulted a very wise-appearing borzoi in the neighborhood. Finally, he comes up with his bet after realizing that one choice stood out from the rest. Advised to look for the blown-out Pekingese, Mr. Truman Paul, to grab the headlines and so makes a visit to his friends at *The View* and *Good Morning America* to revel in the lucrative endorsement contracts on Wednesday morning.

MOST HEARD PHRASES AROUND THE DOG SHOW GROUNDS

"This is one incredible bitch," gets said a lot to describe a very impressive female dog. Kids are advised only to use the term in reference to a dog, to avoid an uncomfortable discussion at school regarding comments to the lunch lady.

"She was Best in Breed, AHHH!" is exclaimed by participants if their dog was the top dog of that particular breed and is allowed to move forward in the judging to Best in Show.

"My win record is on track," is the goal of all dog show participants with a pulse and means you are likely going to be visiting New York in February. An alternative phrase is, "I'm going to the big dance, bitches!"

"Just bait her," refers to a bite-sized treat, perhaps a bit of liver or cheese, to get your dog's attention in the ring.

"This is a benched show." A benched show requires the dogs to stay in an assigned benching area for the length of the show when they are not being shown, groomed, or exercised. The idea is to allow the likes of the Joneses to see the dogs up close and talk to you, the breeders, owners, and handlers.

"That dog." Around the ring, "dog" means male and since dog shows serve as an exhibition of breeding stock, the distinction is vital for obvious reasons.

"My dog is in the working group." The dog does not have to punch a time clock and is free each day to conduct his carefree life. Dogs are grouped into one of seven categories according to the jobs for which the breeds were originally created. Sporting, Hound, Working, Non-Sporting Nerds, Herding, Rat Killing, Prisoner Control, and Juggling are the groups that are featured.

"Stack him." To stack a dog is to cause him to pose in a way that best displays his strong points to the judge. If you use your hands it is "hand stacking;" without hands is "free stacking." If you use your feet it is called "feet stacking," and without feet is called "falling to the ground."

"Zut alors!" Literally translated as "damn so" from French and often heard when your dog or bitch does not see the index finger wag and you are out—no do-overs, mulligans or otherwise; it's pack it in, express *zut alors* and try to hold off your watery, itchy eyes until after you congratulate the victor and begin your journey home. The Beatles' John Lennon used the words *zut alors* in two songs and also an anagram using those letters, "sro tuzla," which led to the belief that this was a reference to LSD or that he was taking LSD.

PREPARING TO SHOW

Do you really want to compete your dog? This is not a decision to make without serious consideration or an ability to pay the high entry fee. Of course, it would be nice to have a wall of ribbons, and a dog with a consistently smooth silky coat and frumpy groupies. It's fulfilling to join a community with the same obsessive dedication to being the best at something really unique and weird.

The preparation can take years and years off of your life, which may actually be dog years. Showing is the key word and everything will need to revolve around the exhibition. Dogs have to constantly look the part, be constantly in training for the part, and be driven around the nation and maybe the globe to show the rest of the world that they do act and look the part, all the while causing a hefty dent in your pocket book (some estimate this may exceed $250,000 annually) and ensuring that you don't have any other hobbies other than TikTok dance videos. You may even forego having children that actually grow up and don't use the yard as a toilet.

The pedigree is paramount. The purpose of dog shows is to maintain the breed standards. Any taint to a bloodline runs contrary to the Kennel Club ethos. The Kennel Club exists to maintain the purity of bloodlines for the betterment of society, or so they think.

SHOULD I SHOW MY DOG?

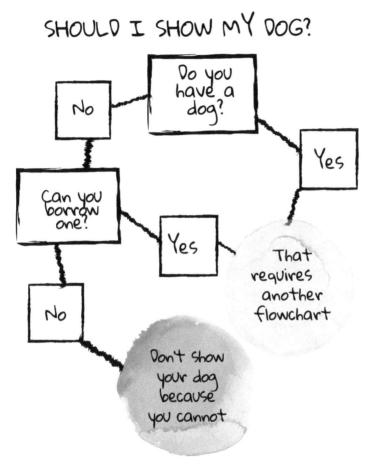

The process of canine race indoctrination has its uncomfortable aspects: pugs that lose eyeballs, breed standards that are thought to be gospel, and discrimination against any deficiency or mixed breed. (There are rumors that such standards are causing deformity. The first clue is when any breed of animal loses its eyeballs.)

If you do decide that you have the dedication and determination, then it's important to choose the most suitable showing category. Things you cannot change like your breed and breed characteristics will dictate how you compete. Choose carefully—you are stuck with your group longer than most people are stuck with their spouse.

GROOMING DIFFICULTLY SCALE

Easy

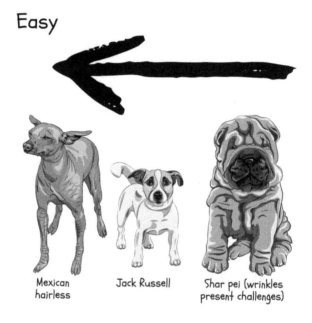

Mexican hairless | Jack Russell | Shar pei (wrinkles present challenges)

TOP CONSIDERATIONS FOR SELECTING A SHOWING CATEGORY

Breed. The road to Best in Show starts with winning the Best in Breed competition. Only the Best in Breed winners advance to compete in the group competitions. As mentioned above, each AKC-recognized breed falls into one of seven group classifications. Some characteristics such as training difficulty seen in certain terriers may be harder to muscle into a pose as compared to a whip-smart workaholic like a border collie that may be telling you to go at it a bit harder.

Additional factors to consider include the investment in grooming required. The nice, easily groomable coat of a terrier may offset the additional hours you need to work on obedience. Whereas, with the puli, whose corded coat some may consider to be as hands off as the hippie family down the street's dreadlocks, you will need to invest hours in rinsing after

Requires greater proficiency and patience or $$$

Labrador (oils on skin and affinity for pond water present challenges)

Golden retriever

Puli (dreadlocks are both cool and a bitch)

a bath to ensure all shampoo has been rinsed away from each dreadlock. Generally, a puli coat takes several hours to dry with a blow dryer, or a few days on its own. And the frustration may cause you to make friends with the budtenders at your local dispensary (if you are not already).

Group. The group is a natural progression from the breed you select, and most groups will be heavily oriented to reflect the tendencies of their handlers. The seven groups are Sporting, Booze Hound, Working, Terrier, Toy, Non-Sporting, and Silent Farting. Four placements are awarded in each group, but only the first-place winner advances to the Best in Show competition. You may think that if you choose a less popular group you have more chances—who shows sheepdogs, right? This is not the case and the points system has a way of equivocating the road to Best in Show.

Odds. Labrador and golden retrievers, although wildly popular nationwide and the people's champion, have never been Westminster Champion and won Best in Show. A clear case of breedism. Perhaps surprisingly, of the 112 Best in Show titles awarded at Westminster, 47—more than 40 percent—have been won by the terrier group. Wire fox terriers alone have won 15 times, more any other breed. Despite the significant odds that make bookies in Vegas buy a new visor, one needs to consider if getting a wire fox terrier will increase the odds of getting the coveted title or not. The announcement of King as winner of Best in Show in 2019 was met with boos and grumbles in Madison Square Gardens, as the dog show world struggled with terrier fatigue and jealousy. King's response was, "When you're good, you're good," and, "You really like me, you really like me.

CHAPTER 12

DOGGY DONATIONS: USING YOUR ADORABLE'S PLATFORM FOR GOOD

A WORLD OF NEW OPPORTUNITIES

A whole new dimension of charitable causes comes forth when you have a dog. As your natural attention moves from the maladies of Africa, expect to be preoccupied with the causes of no-kill shelters and the amazing work of dog rescue organizations and even other animal causes. If your pet can raise money for an elderly elephant in a zoo that doesn't have enough money to buy 500-pound bags of hay or large shovels, it's a game-changer. Of course, this new charitable focus is a reflection of your love of pets but also an obvious way to reveal to all the fabulousness of yours.

There is a plethora of areas where pets and their welfare need your assistance and your Adorable could be the featured donor! Various regular contributions will suffice without the need to become the president of the charity. Here are some ways that you can do good and at the same time your dog can be the centerpiece of charitable giving (check with your tax advisor).

1. **Donate.** Fundraising is the base of all charitable activities. Money makes the good deeds possible. To obtain the funds, organizations may hold auctions, running races, pet walks, brick campaigns and more. Donating money, auction items, or prizes for the run can all be done in the name of your pet. He can even be the one to give out the prize and can surely be the one mentioned by the auctioneer as the donor in the not-so-silent auction. Note: do not auction personal appearances as those can be very stressful to your puppy and winners typically make great demands. On the other hand it can be quite gratifying when the professionally trained auctioneer starts to slow as the bidding gets to a record high due to your Adorable's adorableness. An oft loved campaign by charitable organizations is the brick campaign. Participating will provide a permanent memorial of your dog's generosity and thoughtfulness in the form of a brick or wall tile clearly indicating his name (and an endearing proverb, of course).

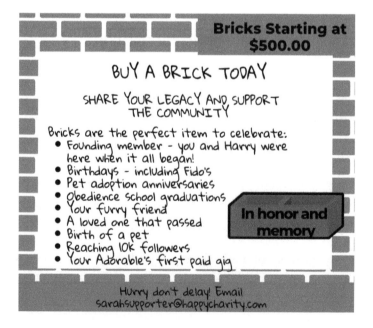

Bricks Starting at $500.00

BUY A BRICK TODAY

SHARE YOUR LEGACY AND SUPPORT THE COMMUNITY

Bricks are the perfect item to celebrate:
- Founding member - you and Harry were here when it all began!
- Birthdays - including Fido's
- Pet adoption anniversaries
- Obedience school graduations
- Your furry friend
- A loved one that passed
- Birth of a pet
- Reaching 10k followers
- Your Adorable's first paid gig

In honor and memory

Hurry don't delay! Email sarahsupporter@happycharity.com

Brick Campaign Samples:

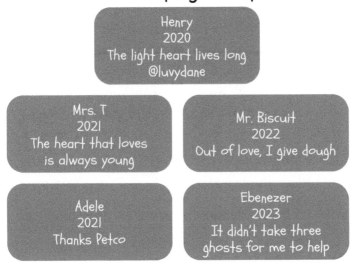

Henry
2020
The light heart lives long
@luvydane

Mrs. T
2021
The heart that loves
is always young

Mr. Biscuit
2022
Out of love, I give dough

Adele
2021
Thanks Petco

Ebenezer
2023
It didn't take three
ghosts for me to help

2. **Foster.** Many shelters yearn for great foster homes, a staging area for adoptable dogs. Fostering is an awesome way for your pet pal to show a newbie the ropes and in the process get extra cute footage of doing good. After all, you have the perfect pet home, and can put those photo skills to the test. There's always the chance that an inadvertent "sidekick" duo is born out of this contribution.

@harryandbalou FOLLOW ···

143 likes
These guys love each other!
They even share food
#puppybesties

3. **Spend for a Cause.** Some rescue organizations, such as Gentle Giants, have a small ecommerce site at which sales support the organization's good deeds. Buy some of these items and use your dog's fame to promote the organization, tag them in posts, and include them in stories. If your dog can fit inside of any of the branded items that are purchasable—a mug, thermos, bowl, skateboard, or Jet Ski—the return is even higher. With your dog at the center, the organization's story will gain awareness, which will naturally lead to more donations.

@harrygives FOLLOW •••

Check out my new collar from Shine for Dogs. 100% of the proceeds go to dogs in rescues and shelters #doinggoodwhilelookinggood

4. **Feature Pet Success Stories.** The rescued rescue the rescue site. Pretty much every rescue site has a success stories section. It may be for pure personal interest but more often than not it's to show that rescued dogs can join a family in perfect harmony. Success stories illustrate that it's not necessary to import a family pet from Germany

to have a faithful companion. If your dog is a rescue, let the rescue center know that he has turned out to be a perfect guy and is loved by all. By promoting rescues and including pictures of your new Adorable that serve as testament to your own rescue success you'll gain thousands of appreciative followers so don't forget to add your IG handle where fans can see all your Adorable's latest feats and cuteness on a daily basis. #whorescuedwho

5. **Search and Rescue.** Dogs' amazing senses make it possible for them to transform from adoring dog into a real-life hero. Search and rescue dogs have won medals and accolades for their work rescuing people and animals from natural disasters and mass casualty events. They are critical to locating and providing aid to those in need. Dogs can sense danger, earthquakes, and five percent shifts in the NAS-DAQ. Your heroic dog may be eligible to receive the highest honors, such as the Animals in War and Peace Medal of Bravery, awarded to any animal displaying conspicuous gallantry and devotion to duty particularly in the armed forces or civil emergency services, or the PDSA Certificate of Animal Bravery or Devotion, which acknowledges the extraordinary bravery and devotion to duty of animals. Not to mention the NYSE award for saving a hedge fund manager's job.

6. **Volunteer as a Therapy Animal.** Giving, not getting. Organizations like the Pet Partners Therapy Animal Program screen and register volunteer therapy animal handlers and their pets to provide safe, effective therapy animal visits in hospitals, assisted living, rehabilitation centers, schools, and other facilities. Imagine the adoration and feelings of goodwill you'll receive from letting others and those most in need of the mutually beneficial human–animal bond. experience the greatness of your dog. A win for all as those assisted will surely become fans and followers. #hairytherapy

In all these instances your furry friend can be at the centerpiece of your charitable efforts, which can be as much about meeting new friends and admirers as doing good work.

@harryhelper [FOLLOW] ...

Stopped in at the hospital today to lift the spirits of those healing #doinggoodforothers

Dear Kendra,

I recently joined Nursing Beyond Borders as it was my fondest hope to participate in their mission to provide healthcare and education to children and their communities on a global scale and to share the love of my Harry with those same children to further the mission.

Unfortunately, I learned right before I was to leave on my first trip abroad that it was against policy for Harry to join me. I am so disappointed as I know Harry could support the mission in an incredibly positive way.

Do you have any suggestions?

Gratefully,
Sad Samaritan

....

Sad Samaritan,

As much as we agree with you about the likelihood of Harry being able to support the mission in a positive way, rules of others are rules. However, all is not lost. This is a fabulous opportunity for you to create your own charitable organization with your own rules (and own tax relief). One suggestion for such an organization is Adorables Beyond Borders. Adorables Beyond Borders could have a remarkably similar mission since we are all very aware of the science supported positive benefits of our furry friends on health.

This makes the most sense as what are you supposed to do, leave Harry at home? He simply needs to be, and should be, part of any charitable efforts.

Thank you for your contributions,

Kendra

FOR THE ORGANIZER AT HEART

If you don't want to simply make a donation there is a host of other great ideas that you can spearhead that will garner donation funds and publicity for the cause and your deserving Adorable. Here is a list of some of the better prospects that Adorables and charities have appreciated being a part of.

Pet Talent Show. Most pet owners like to show off their pet's tricks, which can be the source of success if the zealousness of certain acts is tempered. Some auditions and pre-screening may be necessary to ensure that high quality standards are maintained that will draw a crowd in years to come for this sure-to-be annual event. Money is earned through entry fees and a small fee for spectators. All proceeds can be donated to your favorite charity.

Halloween Ball. For some, images of inappropriate masquerade balls may come to mind, but this would be a far lighter sort of fest and involve costume contests and other fun Halloween events for dogs and their friends alike. Money received through donations and admissions can be donated to your favorite pet cause.

Charity Auction. The fast pace of a live auction, a smooth-talking auctioneer, peer pressure, and alcohol are usually cause for an 80 percent increase in paddle waving. Add to that a pet cause that will be discussed in the most heartfelt manner prior to the auction starting and you have a sure-fire winner.

Custom T-Shirt Sales. T-shirt-making is the easy part; it's flogging them that's difficult. This is especially true if you

1. Find location and get approval.

Do not leave out the fact that the participants are pets! Make sure venue can hold a lot of people due to the inevitable popularity.

2. Set a date!

Avoid booking on holidays unless your show will be the feature of the holidays, which is perfectly reasonable

3. Make a budget

You will always need money so figure out how to get others to pay for your idea with sponsorships or get Harry to teach you how to beg.

4. Sell tickets.

Avoid targeting selling efforts on participants and children and direct efforts to those with money and lots of friends.

5. Find a Celebrity.

Celebrity should assist with event publicity. Celebrity can be a pet or human and even your pet! (benefit of being organizer)

6. Ensure attendees' happiness

Supervise volunteers and ensure event is special so that you can repeat for years to come!

decide to create T-shirts for pets that are adorned with "I'm with Stupid." Don't forget that the one with the wallet is often not the dog.

Viral Challenge. Although we throw the term viral around carefully these days, there is no replacement for a challenge that catches on à la the ice bucket challenge, the success of which is now the goal of all challenges. Challenges are a great way to raise awareness and the pet set is the perfect audience. If their pet does not accept the challenge to balance a treat on their nose or something similarly cute while being recorded, they must pay up, and if they do the challenge, they may make a donation anyway.

Create a Pet Animal Calendar. Not only can this be a great holiday gift, but it also provides the opportunity for additional fandom for your Adorable Just remember the hottest calendar pin-ups are usually December—you will want to reserve that spot for your Adorable.

Photo Contest. This is another one where you can do good *and* get some stellar PR for your Adorable. These tend to be competitive so up your game, have some great prizes, and ensure that the judges are properly compensated.

CHAPTER 13

A STAR IS BORN: A DOG'S ROLE IN MEDIA AND ENTERTAINMENT

THE ADORABLE PANTHEON—A COLLECTION OF THE MOST BELOVED ADORABLES

Some well-known Adorables, both fictional and real, have become permanent inhabitants of our joint consciousness. These beloved Adorables are part of a pantheon that both inspire and instruct.

Elevation to the Adorable Pantheon is an honor not only bestowed on those Adorables that have reached true celebrity status, but also on those that have transcended a 10k following on IG or from a viral video. These dogs have made their Adorableness into a full-time occupation, not just a means to expand a fan base, and they therefore instruct and inspire us.

THE ROLL CALL:

LASSIE

The TV dog played by over 100 Collies in the show's run (the many changes were due to contract disputes and weight gain issues). Lassie showed the importance of a dog in weekly rescue operations where random members of her community fell down the same mineshaft. Her ability to completely communicate a tragic situation perfectly for a 12-year-old boy to understand and alert the proper authorities was astounding. This talent locked into the world's psyche the importance of a dog, a fact that had been merely hinted at in the previous thousands of years of dog ownership.

SCOOBY AND SHAGGY

Scooby needs no introduction as the loyal sidekick to Shaggy that took on many of his personality traits. He inspired and instructed by normalizing dog detectives and co-dependence with your dog. In addition, despite Scooby's less than perfect off-breed features, including a double chin, bowed legs, and spots as opposed to a clean, even coat, he was equally endearing if not more so, than the typical. Since the inception of the show, the number of pups becoming full-time detectives has doubled.

BRUISER AND ELLE

Bruiser, the near silent co-star of *Legally Blonde* and Elle's sidekick, was a loving ear as Elle transformed her stereotypes into success. Bruiser educated and inspired us by causing us to consider that pre-judging others can bite you in the ass (including Chihuahuas) and that Chihuahuas are completely acceptable, along with pink and high heels, as opposed to being impediments to brains and achievements. Some even say that Bruiser birthed the "Dog in Handbag" movement. Some movie trivia: the producers had originally planned for Bruiser to have a mini handbag with an even tinier Adorable inside but abandoned the idea due to budgetary constraints.

ASTRO FROM *THE JETSONS*

Astro, the loyal pal of the Jetson family, made the Adorable Pantheon for inspiring and instructing us about dogs in the future. Astro was one of the first dogs in the media to understand and speak English, which makes sense given the show was set in the future and gave all confidence that despite flying cars, canine companionship will be just as necessary in the future as it is today. Unlike most futuristic shows, not one invention ever became a reality except for the Tesla bag.

BRIAN FROM *FAMILY GUY*

Brian Griffin, the dog star of *Family Guy*, has served as evening entertainment for years. Brian made the list for different reasons than most portrayals of the traditional loyal pets in media, namely for his intelligence. Brian is college educated and cultured. He upped the ante for dogs and when we are having a full conversation with our own dogs, we can all think of Brian. Dogs can be smarter than humans: the latest scientific testing put that number at 40 percent.

CLIFFORD, THE BIG RED DOG

Clifford the big red dog, as his name suggests, has entertained us for years with his best friend, eight-year-old Emily Elizabeth, who frequently rides and climbs on her gigantic, and at times, clumsy, but gentle companion. Clifford readily deserves a place in the Adorable Pantheon for his ability to inform and inspire us, though often causing angst in the process. Unconditional love of dogs and their humans prevails over any incident related to clumsiness that may or may not have caused some real destruction. And besides, big dogs are cool.

EDDIE FROM *FRASIER*

Eddie, played by Moose on *Frasier*, reached Pantheon status quickly not just for his obvious cult following but by informing us that our psychiatrists are not all-knowing. If Eddie could bait ultra-control-freak psychiatrist Frasier, we too have a chance. Also, he showed us that when our dogs run the house, we don't need to feel bad.

FLASH FROM THE DUKES OF HAZZARD

Flash, nicknamed Velvet Ears, joined the show three years in but was a popular addition to the storyline in that she too had a distaste for Boss Hogg. Flash educated and inspired us not because it was one of the first times that we saw a basset hound on TV but because we were able to see what we had always known about dogs in action: dogs are typically on the right side of the law and a recognizable pet superpower is the ability to distinguish between good and evil.

SNOOPY

Snoopy, the beagle from *Peanuts* was known as "the hip dog we'd all like to be."

Snoopy inspired us as we realized that dogs can be funnier than humans and that is okay. Humans can still take pleasure in the fact that they are funnier than Garfield.

Dogs in Media Reaching Our Subconscious

The media infiltrates our consciousness with their messages at every turn. For dogs this has been quite positive. Dogs in the media typically play a positive role; they may have bad behavior such as Marley in *Marley & Me* but in the end the dog is endearing, helpful, and loyal and tugs your heart-strings enough that you find yourself cruising adoption sites and making arrangements to get your own. Those who have been spurred into action to become a Shaggy or a deserving family of a Beethoven rejoice that the media has reserved its negative, unrealistic, stereotypical, and limiting perceptions to women and minorities and left the positive attributions of dogs to nicely infiltrate into our subconscious.

ADORABLES IN ENTERTAINMENT-THE BEHIND-THE-SCENES TRUE STORY

CELEBRITY OWNERS KEEPING MEMORIES ALIVE

Celebrities are fodder for pushing the limits as they have the creativity and means to do things that may not be possible for others. These traits do not escape the world of dogs and their owners' desire to preserve their doggie relationship postmortem. Here are some ways they have found to never let go when their dogs pass. If you have trouble deciding which to emulate consider engaging a death doula, certified and trained at the University of Vermont Companion Animal End of Life Doula program.

Doulas can assist with the overwhelming decisions that come with the end of life that you may have had to navigate with a relative or friend without support. There are nationwide doula franchises available that have exploded at tradeshows with their catchy slogan, "Nothing is Coola than Being an End-of-Life Doula."

CLONING DOGS

Forget a cute picture; a cloned dog allows fans of Adorables to preserve their relationships for another dog lifecycle. Genetically a twin of the donor dog, cloned dogs share many attributes including temperament, intelligence, and appearance. Barbra Streisand honored the death of her beloved Coton de Tulear, Samantha, by cloning her into Miss Scarlett and Miss Violet.

Simon Cowell asserts that he is going to clone his dogs as he cannot bear not having them around, even suggesting that he may do it now, which would double the number of dogs in his care from three to six. This could be a bit much for anyone to keep up with, even one accustomed to judging others with a keen eye. Clearly, neither Barbra nor Simon have ever watched a movie about cloning that warns of faulty copies becoming homicidal maniacs. Everyone would be very sad if a clone killed Barbra.

CRYOPRESERVATION

Cryonics is a technique intended to extend lifespan by cooling legally dead dogs to liquid nitrogen temperature where physical decay essentially stops, in the hope that future scientific procedures will someday revive them and restore them to youth and good health. A dog held in such a state is said to be a "cryopreserved patient," because those in the cryo world do not regard the cryopreserved as being inevitably "dead" If you choose cryopreservation for your Adorable, some cryonic tank farms require you to buy a package for yourself as well. It would be pointless and rather confusing, after all, to have your Adorable among the living in years to come without you by his side. Most cryo personnel don't mention that your dog and you will have to live with side effects. The most obvious being that after regeneration you stay the color blue.

ASHES

While some opt for cremation and find it comforting to be near their cremated or to spread them on their favorite hiking trail, others go further afield, like Drew Barrymore, who took her dear Flossie's ashes to India to scatter. Her stops: Gandhi's house in New Delhi, a Buddhist monastery up in the Himalayas, and a quiet path in the countryside by the Ganges River. I am not certain if those were Flossie's favorite spots but the decision to cremate and where to spread the ashes are all personal.

TATTOOS

Unlike your current boyfriend's name, the permanency of a tattoo featuring your pet is of no concern, which made tattoos no-brainers for remembering a lost one for the likes of Miley Cyrus, Jennifer Aniston, Pink, Howard Stern, and other celebrities who have commemorated their deceased dogs in ink. Celebrities tend to follow certain tattoo artists like a cult, which reveals that if you elect to go down this route, the artist may be as important as the decision so as not to have your Adorable looking any less Adorable than IRL.

FREEZE-DRYING

Speaking of IRL, freeze-drying can do just that. It will retain your pet in all his glory, life-sized, and able to have the odd chat with you (knowing there will be no tail wag or bark in return). Freeze-drying removes liquid and moisture from an object that is frozen by using a slow vacuum process and once this process is complete the pet you love so much will be with you forever, or at least appear that way.

PORTRAITS

Portrait artists can provide a comforting rendition of your pet while also contributing to the look and feel of your home or office. Some even specialize in immortalizing your pet in certain themes, like the Renaissance. Aunt Sally will understand when she gets displaced from the mantle for a life-size of your Adorable; it will be up to you to decide whether a joker outfit is appropriate.

Dog-Lover Oprah.

Most dogs at one time: 11

Famous Oprah dog quote: "Nothing makes me happier than being with my dogs. Sorry, Stedman. Dogs prevail."

Ritual: All her dogs send her flowers on her birthday

Dog trust fund: Purportedly $30m

Oprah's out-of-touch-with-reality rating: 8 out of 10 stars

CHAPTER 14

ADORABLE CELEBRATIONS FOR EVERY PUP SEASON

Holidays and the change of season are the perfect time to demonstrate adoration and love; there's nothing better than a pet adorned with seasonally themed wear. The attention they attract during the holidays shines on them, reflects back to you, then shines back on them: your puppy is a gift that keeps on giving and receiving. This is the perpetual attention motion machine that can drive emotional profits for the rest of the year.

Tradition relative to each family will inform how holidays are spent and the graciousness with which your dog is included by third-party family members. It is incumbent on all involved in holiday celebrations to be on their best behavior. With proper preparation, inclusion is guaranteed and focus can be turned to the seasonal celebration at hand.

Unfortunately, and although not typical, any missteps by Harry will be more memorable than Aunt Mildred's inappropriate comments about her new lover in assisted living (since those are expected and are of no surprise to anyone).

YOUR ADORABLE AND THE FOOTBALL GAME

"Puperee"
Already adorns glasses as offensive
measure for certain comments
related to getting improved
eyesight even though eyesight is
20/75 (better than humans')

"Pupticipant"
Sometimes results in winner claiming
"Deflategate" with later dispute
rivaling a similar issue in the NFL
(although any pressure issue is
unintentional) which affects familial
relations for the weekend

THANKSGIVING

The cornucopia of connection. The marker of mid-fall and the longest running break from obligations for you and others to enjoy your dog and his stellar company. (This holiday of attention is the set-up to the Christmas spike.)

Thanksgiving is the holiday most likely to result in an invitation to a third-party home to partake in festivities with others who may not yet be aware of Harry's adorableness. Some may think that Thanksgiving is a holiday only for the two-legged, but not so. It brings many opportunities, but also potential pitfalls, for our furry companions, too.

Opportunities to steal the show include: adored mascot of family football game, lap dog while sports viewing, and superior cleaner of spills and leftovers. There is some debate over whether, during a long touchdown run, barking with the cheering family or silently running around the room as the play unwinds is the most satisfying. Our opinion is to train them to do what comes easiest. Note: once a dog crosses 80 pounds this entire exercise is out the window.

Opportunities for pitfalls that may result in a revoking of repeat invitations include: causing spills, eating unmanned food, begging at the dinner table, and an 80-pound dog barking and running in circles to a long touchdown run.

WINTER HOLIDAYS

More than ugly sweaters for your crowd. With the winter holiday comes more parties and, of course, opportunities to show off your Adorable in a cheery atmosphere. Festivities have the potential to amplify cuteness perceptions tenfold due to the backdrop and swag itself but also thanks to the gracious, kind-hearted attitudes brought about by the holidays—along

GIFT GIVING

Participation Options for Pups

Present Delivery
(Soft Mouth Is Critical)

Be The Present
(Human Favorite)

Receive the Present
(Dog Favorite)

Unwrap the Present
(For those with weary fingers)

with the spiked eggnog. For some, the primary focus of the season is religious gatherings, which are usually unattended by Adorables, unlike other parties and celebrations.

Nevertheless, the holiday season is packed with opportunities for your Adorable to reveal his adorableness and with the chance for you to document such adorableness. Imagine: you and your Adorable with matching ugly sweaters; your Adorable in his antler headband or Santa Hat (this truly depends on your dog but is a great photo opportunity); your Adorable as the feature on photo ornaments or your family holiday card. You must work hard throughout the year to ensure that your Adorable's 's performance as Santa's helper delivering presents on Christmas morning goes off without a hitch. No potential fan can resist a present delivery of a fabulous gift from a fabulous dog.

As we know, every opportunity brings with it the same associated potential pitfalls. Any performance can go awry with a misstep. Since the season is focused on religious celebrations and has a heavy emphasis on giving and home decorations, interference with either of these will amplify the negative perception of your Adorable's behavior.

Any sort of destruction of the Christmas tree, including peeing on it, chewing ornaments or lights, and knocking them off with careless ignorance of their preciousness; any destruction of religious relics like having a chew on the Nativity scene even though the manger may be irresistible; abusing any other home decoration; and finally, assisting with unwrapping presents prior to Christmas morning, which is most unwelcome and to be avoided at all costs. Remember the old adage regarding the karmic likelihood that the thing your dog destroys will have been made by a deceased relative.

WHITE ELEPHANT GIFT SELECTIONS

This year your pet pals, two-legged and four-legged alike, have infiltrated this classic holiday tradition and opted for a pet gift exchange. Match the white elephant gift with the pet most likely to have brought it to the party.

Mastiff	New tennis ball
Retriever Mix	Steak (raw or cooked)
Hound Mix	Toy squirrel (with squeaker)
Rat terrier	Bacon treats (the stronger the smell the better)
Pomeranian	Bedazzler
Chow Chow	Tickets to anger management seminar
Papillon	Comfy pillow (the larger the better)
Great Dane	Chia pet lookalike

For anyone unfamiliar with certain breed characteristics or just not as imaginative a shopper as your Adorable, the answers are:
Mastiff – steak,
Hound Mix – bacon treats,
Chow Chow – tickets to anger management seminar,
Retriever Mix – tennis balls,
Rat Terrier – toy squirrel
Papillon – bedazzler,
Great Dane – comfy pillow,
Pomeranian – chia pet lookalike

HANUKKAH

Hanukkah is a blessing in the world of Adorables, not just because it marks an additional celebratory event with a certain role for an Adorable but because it lasts eight whole days!

Since Hanukkah isn't traditionally a big gift-giving holiday, your Adorable should not expect a new toy selection; rather, Adorables are normally given "gelt" (which means money in Yiddish): coins or small gifts of money from family members.

While some families of Adorables give gifts to help their Adorables fit in during Christmas time, which bolsters the gift-giving memory creation discussed above, others nowadays are pushing back against consumerism by giving fewer gifts or by opting for experiences instead of objects, which is fine with most and presents even greater opportunities to memorialize the holiday.

Thankfully, some communities have designated the fifth night of Hanukkah (the night when the majority of candles are lit) specifically for giving to others, volunteering, or making donations (see Charity section). This offers a potential role for your Adorable but really any shot with your Adorable volunteering and helping the community during Hanukkah will be an excellent commemorative holiday shot. #fifthnightservice

WINTER OUTDOOR FUN

The December holiday season is not just for social celebrations; it's also an opportunity for outdoor activities in the snow with your Adorable. This may mean a backcountry ski, snowball fight, or snowshoeing. Charges of Adorables proceed with caution when it comes to enjoying snow activities with their pals. Many parks with the best snow have a no-dog policy, which can make skiing incredibly dog unfriendly.

SNOW INSPO FROM OUTDOOR ENTHUSIAST DOG IG ACCOUNTS

There will be many opportunities for Harry to shine in a snow environment. Consider clothing and gear props, goggles (please), and cute images of snow play. Steal some imagery and activity inspo from these outdoor experts.

@alexborsuk and Otto. Otto made his Instagram debut from a backpack. Now sans backpack and all grown up Otto joins Alex on every jaw-dropping and appropriate ski tour and backcountry hiking adventure. You may not be Alex, but your dog can be Otto, or a form of him.

@officialsnowdog is the handle of an expert winter Burmese mountain outdoor dog and his engaging imagery supports the title. Parker supports PR efforts at the dog-friendly Loveland Ski Area along with many other charitable causes. His antics are always documented and he can be seen lending a helping paw to the Loveland snowmaking team, riding around in the snow cat, and simply looking adorable in his snow goggles. You may not have access to a snow cat, but you can work with the others.

@andrew_muse and @Kickerdogmuse. The accounts of both the pals of this dynamic duo are full of well-curated imagery of outdoor fun and adventure, including snow play. These two appear to live the van life and are often seen taking on year-round adventure. The feature footage of Kicker, a golden retriever, charging at powdery mountains, is inspirational. Kicker clearly loves snow, specifically digging holes in it.

SNOW PRO TIPS FOR ADORABLES

Keep warm.

@alexborsuk is never in the backcountry without a puffer and booties for her pal. She always has treats and snacks for refueling, which may contribute to staying warm as well.

Pesky snowballs in the fur?

Bothered by snowballs that collect on their paws and belly? Spray your dog's paws and belly with cooking spray before you head out to keep snowballs at bay.

Stay visible.

Not only does a cute bright coat or collar make a snow photo pop, it also makes your dog easier to see in the backcountry.

SPRING VACATION

Fort Liquordale and Harry? Hardly. Spring break, oft considered a college rite of passage of days filled with drunken disorderliness in Panama City, South Padre, or Cancun, is not really representative of Harry's destination ideal or his true set. Thank goodness the vacation has progressed. More appropriate venues may be hiking the Poconos, or a lake or beach excursion.

Either way fans will appreciate some new content to mark the changing seasons: blooming trees and flowers along with park play against a spring setting is perfect for that.

Spring also marks Easter! The Easter Bunny never forgets an Adorable so this is the perfect opportunity for you to bring out the bunny ears and Easter basket. Some Adorables have found themselves in hot water at this time of year by raiding Easter baskets and prematurely taking part in the egg hunt before the children of the household or town. Typically, they live through the chocolate experience but may not survive the bad press of angry parents and organizers.

When your Adorable asks to go out on Easter morning, he needs supervision. For some reason, although he has been unable to find the ball stashed in the rosemary for the last month, he sniffs out the plastic eggs in the same place within minutes. If he makes it through these pitfalls, he can be more revered for his cuteness than an actual encounter with the Easter Bunny himself.

Harry's Easter Basket

Most Easter baskets are focused on chocolate and sugar, which is even less ideal for Adorables than for children. We found some alternatives that will be equally appealing but not as toxic.

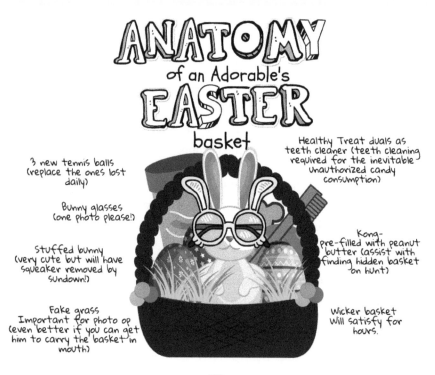

ANATOMY of an Adorable's EASTER basket

Healthy Treat duals as teeth cleaner (teeth cleaning required for the inevitable unauthorized candy consumption)

3 new tennis balls (replace the ones lost daily)

Bunny glasses (one photo please!)

Kong- pre-filled with peanut butter (assist with finding hidden basket on hunt)

Stuffed bunny (very cute but will have squeaker removed by sundown!)

Fake grass Important for photo op (even better if you can get him to carry the basket in mouth)

Wicker basket Will satisfy for hours.

SUMMER

Adorables embrace summer. For most, it means sitting, playing, picnic and barbecue scraps, parades, hiking, and beach fun with their pal. Summer travel also brings a wealth of opportunities to exhibit adorableness along with the carefree nature of the season (and no pesky outerwear). Possible excursions can be road trips to some place dog-friendly (check the park rules) or a beach, lake, or river house that provides endless hours of walks, throws, and swims. The mountains are another option although they're usually reserved for sporty types.

Summer is the high point of most dogs' entire year. The time when puppies blossom into mature dogs and a reference point for the beginning of many life skills: "Remember the summer when Harry learned to swim?" Fond memories of beach fires, lazy evening games of throw, barbecues and beer, a visit to a baseball game, or a drive-in movie keep spirits up through the other seasons until the next holiday arrives.

Your photography of these fond moments will later adorn your home and social media and get reintroduced on IG whenever there is a dry spell for posting interest or when long winter days become unbearable. (Note: long winter days are perfect for extra exercise and community involvement. Ignoring these two important healthy habits is the same as a dog smoking two packs of cigarettes a day. Cigarette photos aren't recommended.)

@Happygolucky [FOLLOW] ⋯

Summer fun at the drive-in. Who is with me with the thought that Devil Dog did not really need to be a movie?
#driveinmovie #fanunfavorite

Harry is the hit of any parade – bonus if he drives the car

PARADE PARTICIPANT!

Adorables love parades and the Fourth of July parade steals the show in most small towns. Parade participants will likely seek your Adorable out to ride shotgun in their convertible classic car, AKA parade float. Naturally, your Adorable should be the ride-along guest of the Mayor or the hit of some other float, preferably a cool one like a military-issued tank that arrived in your town of 5,000 for some reason or one that throws candy from it so it will be sure to garner the most attention. What Adorables must avoid in the parade is walking. Walking in parades is for boy scouts and bands; Adorables need to have the wind in their hair and be at spectators' eye level and only a float or vehicle can provide that. Almost too obvious as an Adorable visual is the bike basket, which, strangely, works every year and at any time. The bike was invented in the 1800s and a dog in a basket was invented one hour later. This fact calls to mind the question: Why in the world did it take so long?

The ambitious also choose the summer season to polish certain skills such as swimming, trying out a new trick or agility, and brushing up on obedience. Not only is the practice environment perfect but summer presents itself with a ton of opportunities to test those skills: think any function with a built-in audience like barbecues and beach parties and if swimming has been the focus of the summer, the end-of-season Dog in the Pool swim will be a great spot to reveal your Adorable's new-found athleticism.

SWIMMING

The Dog in the Pool event is a long-standing tradition that marks the end of summer with a dog celebration. Public pools across the nation allow dogs in the pool for the last swim day of the year prior to closing the pool in the fall. Towns like Atlanta, Los Angeles, and Seattle aptly name these celebrations Doggie Splash, Doggie Paddle, and Paws in the Pool. A town can be measured on its dog friendliness based on the offering and quality of a Dog in the Pool celebration.

@Happygolucky FOLLOW ...

Dog Splash with pals! Stay safe and have fun!
#dogdaysofsummer

COOL PARTY TRICK SKETCH SERIES.

Your dog can be the hit of the barbecue! (From the *Curious George* playbook: should there ever be a mishap, a clever trick or good deed is always the way to recover.) Most dogs rely on a few scraps at barbecues and picnics, but tricks are a way to get him the real goods and to show off his talents.

"Go fetch a beer!" This will depend on your storage space, cooler, or fridge. If you intend to show off with a fridge then you need to train at home with a fridge and likewise with a cooler. You might find a dedicated drinks fridge to be preferable since your dog could get distracted with the other dishes on offer, creating certain challenges to pulling this one off without mishap.

Kind request

Dog procures beer from cooler or fridge

PARTY SERIES

Dog transports
(soft mouth required)

Delivery of high
praise and adoration
thereafter

DOG BEER?

Summer is synonymous with a cold beer but tempting as it is, sharing a beverage with your Adorable is not recommended. Don't worry, the entrepreneurial spirit in America is alive and well and brewers have responded to the obvious need and desire we have to share a cold one with our dogs. You can procure select beer offerings just for your Adorable and toast cans in the best company with these options:

Bowser Beer for Dogs. Available in Beefy Brown Ale, Cockadoodle Doo, and Porky Pug Porter.

Pet Winery Barkbrew. All-natural Beef Ale can even be poured into molds to create beersickles.

Good Boy Dog Beer. Offers a variety pack including Crotch Sniffin' Ale, IPA Lot in the Yard, Mailman Malt Likker, and Session…Squirrel.

When you send your Adorable off for a can, he can grab his own too. Both dog and human should caution against swapping brands. This is not like mixing a Coors or a Bud; this mix-up could turn either off a refreshing treat for a while.

HALLOWEEN

Marking the onset of fall, Halloween is full of fodder for dogs, unfortunately not usually in the form of fun activities but rather in kitsch costumes that are unanimously despised by pets. Fall creates a conundrum for those that serve Adorables. For the most part, Adorables are above the costume set and should not be humiliated by being forced to wear a princess costume. However, at the same time a tiara is simply too irresistible. In Halloween celebrations selectivity is critical. Not only does your dog persona require a match, unless the unmatch is completely ironic (think Pekingese in a motorcycle jacket complete with club badges) but the Adorable must maintain his humility and self-respect (for further guidance see Chapter 5 Beautiful Inside and Out: Stellar Accessories for Living the Narrative).

THE COSTUME CONTEST

Winning the Halloween Costume Contest is tough due to the subjective nature of the competition and the diversity of the judges. However, it's possible to "dress to the test," as several criteria are typically used such as most innovative, best homemade, and best store bought. The benefit of entering pets in such competitions is that you don't have to have the typical argument that parents struggle with about the merits of their child *not* choosing their favorite superhero like 10 other kids in the class. Here, you get to be the decider and with that comes the weight of selecting the best costume. There will be no "I told you so" when the judges don't give your Adorable first place—it will be on you. The most consistently successful winning tactic when you don't have time to get too creative is to play against type.

Tiger, a fawn French bulldog, is the reigning champion of the Pawball Halloween Costume Contest. Guess what his winning costume was:

1. Jockey. Complete with custom silks and whip as a prop. Goggles propped on head.

2. Lion. Mane collar. Easy and can stay on without adjustment. Chicken leg dog toy prop placed in mouth during judging.

3. Monkey with banana. Purchased from petcostumecenter.com

4. Luau shirt and offset straw hat.

Winner: Jockey, with its hint of irony. Not available for purchase at petcostumecenter.com so wins points for originality. Sewn by hand by local tailor so lacks cheesy humiliation of other costumes and has colors specifically selected to go with fawn coloring. Has goggle prop but no other difficult flopping props that go unused and detract from the costume. Also, unlike a lion or a monkey, a jockey is not a costume of another animal, which is particularly humiliating since the dog species is superior than the dress-up animal. The Luau shirt does denote fun and a party-like attitude but does not properly reflect or present irony with Tiger's persona.

CHAPTER 15

THE ATHLETIC ADORABLE: SPORTS FOR YOUR PUP

Kareem Abdul Jabbar, as he is known today, NBA's leading scorer, recognized that in high school the sport we play isn't just about winning the game, it's also about defining our individuality among the hundreds of other students in our school. At a young age he recognized that participation in sports was a way to win the admiration of classmates and teachers alike. Similarly, the Sporting Life can define the individuality of your Adorable as well as provide ample content for your IG feed. Strangely, when this high-school sports star finally became a household name, he changed it, from Lew Alcindor to Kareem Abdul Jabbar and unfortunately had to rewalk his path to fame. When you initially pursue a sporty quest for individuality make sure that you're happy with your name as it is.

Those who underestimate the adaptability of Adorables and their human sidekicks may doubt that traditional sports can be practiced with an Adorable in tow. That doubt has no foundation, since the common consensus is that life with an Adorable only gets better. If your friends referred to you

TESTING DOGS'

1. Fill bath

2. Place the dog in the bath

3. Add toys that resemble ocean dwelling species

PROCLIVITY FOR SURFING

4. Place dog on surfboard. Size may be a problem- boogie board may be necessary

5. Leave dog for 20 minutes

Dog in tub on surfboard = proclivity for surfing

Dog in bathroom shaking water everywhere and eating toothbrush = maybe no proclivity for surfing

as "Sporty Spice" before, know that you can now add a Sporty Adorable to most any sport experience. Most standard sports have been adapted to celebrate the participation of Adorables either with competitions dedicated to them or by use of special equipment.

Bringing Your Adorable Along. What you may have previously thought of as solo sports can be adapted so that you never have to leave out your sporty Adorable. Like these popular solo-turned-tandem activities.

Surfing. Hanging 10 with your best friend has great appeal. The sport has numerous competitions, culminating in the World Dog Surfing Championships, which include a focus on surfing and beachwear, making it fodder for documentation. Although it takes an Adorable that is keen on riding the waves, its participants come in all shapes and sizes from pugs to Bostons to goldens. Events include solo dog riding and tandem riding. Surfing is an event with double viral potential: once for appearing on @worlddogsurfingchampionships and another for your own account.

SUCCESSFUL BIKING WITH YOUR ADORABLE

Nice scenery

Good weather

Adorable safe and secure away from bike spokes

No flat tires

Road not too rough for rears of both

True tail World Dog Surfing Championships competitors @starfishthe-rat, @roxy.the.surfing.boston, and @lilylilothelab were co-Grand Marshals at Fog Fest in Pacifica due to their surfing prowess. If you are ready to hang ten with your best friend pick up a copy of a *Dog's Guide to Surfing* or attend a surf camp. Both should top of the list prior to hitting the world tour.

Biking. Don't get caught in the spokes. Who needs an excuse to get to your favorite café faster and avoid long boring walks? Once thought of as a solo activity the market has responded with zeal to the needs of Adorables to be with their humans. Bike carriers for your Adorable, like the Travelin K9 Pet-Pilot Wicker MAX, which includes a wire top with sun-shade will not only ensure that, unlike your own bruised seat, imprinted butt, and sunned face from riding around town, your Adorable is comfortable and shaded. There are also bike trailers out there but these score low marks for Insta-worthiness due to no cute head and paws popping out the front and lack the wind in your face draw of biking. Don't be surprised if your dog is mistaken for your child. This can be funny as well as disconcerting. For the more active Adorables, a bar leash that attaches to your bike allows you to have a seat while your Adorable is pounding the pavement and getting super fit.

Hiking. Hiking provides equal enjoyment for both you and your Adorable and usually happens in some very picturesque places. The view, the typically good weather, and the attire selected for the occasion provide the perfect backdrop for some great images, all while you get fit and healthy and enjoy time with your charge. Your Adorable's stature will dictate whether they are assisting with the load or adding to it but either way hiking is an unquestionable match of fun and resulting gorgeous imagery. Get inspo from @ loki, the leader of the pack on hiking and being sporty in the wilderness with over 2m followers. Watch for narrowing trails or paths that are obscured by dense brush as these can lead to getting lost and/or a movie on the Lifetime Channel.

HIKING LOAD GUIDE
Assist with the Load

Excessive amounts of energy

Has been known to tolerate the odd ride of children

Considered to be of the Working dog group

Strong shoulders and back

Known to enjoy long hikes

Pack will fit - not obese or skinny

*Critical evaluation to avoid having to carry the pack and the dog mid hike. Most doggie backpacks will not fit on people.

Become the Load

Accustomed to being carried in arms, back pack, handbag, or other

Pack not likely to fit (will drag on ground)

Non weight-bearing conformation

Generally unfamiliar with uneven surfaces

Pack not available in mini size

Check out more wisdom about the outdoors at thepopularpets.com

Paddle Board Guide
How to Teach Your Adorable to Paddle Board

Paddle Boarding. Paddle boarding is another solo activity that can include an Adorable. You just need a couple of adjustments to your gear and a little training so that you both don't end up doggie paddling in the bay. Paddle boards range in sizes from smallish to a relative island. Tending toward more island-like features will help when your Adorable decides he needs to scratch that nagging itch in the middle of a lake.

ADORABLE'S FAVORITE DOGA POSES

Warrior

Bridge

Trikonasana

Doga. The Sanskrit meaning of Yoga, "joining," or "uniting" the human spirit with the divine spirit, takes on a new meaning for Adorables and their friends; the divine spirit is in fact the Adorable in a practice called Doga. Doga practitioners rave about creating harmony and synchronization of energy flow between dogs and themselves. Experiences differ—some dogs focus on an opportunity for a playdate with their other pals in the studio, while some are most curious about the treat bribes on offer. Few Adorables will manage to focus on unity and practice downward-facing dog in tandem with their Doga partner for very long.

A word of caution: treats, an essential tool of pose manipulation in Doga and a focus driver, have the potential to result in a waterfall of drool pouring all over a brand-new yoga mat. Your sweaty body, a veritable fur magnet, will be covered in drool and sweat but remember: unity abounds as your canine Zen master looks at you with a relaxed, happy grin, eager to go outside and greet the birds and squirrels in a new state of mindfulness.

To lower your expectations, it's virtually impossible for an Adorable to breathe and clear their mind no matter how many treats you give them as they will always have visions of treats dancing in their heads.

Horse riding. By virtue of its requirement for a horse and more importantly, leash laws, horse riding with your Adorable may be limited to those that live in rural areas. Not suitable for all as Adorables need to walk on their own and be off leash. Nonetheless, it's fun to ride with your dog. If you happen to meet up with the right crew to provide this opportunity just make sure your Adorable won't be tempted to nip the heels of your horse and cause you to return to the ground alongside him.

In Paleolithic times dogs were much larger, and an enemy of the horse. A dog that nears a horse's heels can trigger an instinctive kicking response to avenge horse ancestors brought down by packs. However, if they are able to connect with your little buddy horses have been known to whinny with the sound of diabolical laughter. Dogs seem particularly slow to recognize this behavior due to the distraction of eating horse manure, which puts them directly in the strike zone. Approach this joint sport with caution.

Running. A no-brainer lifetime sport you can do with your Adorable. With the dawn of running belts and leash attachments the chances of getting road rash on your knees from being tripped by the leash is reduced but caution is still advised. Your Adorable stopping to gaze into your eyes for an approving nod can cause a collision just as sure as checking a short text from a friend asking what you are up to while heading at speed towards a stop sign. Additional bonus: if you enjoy running together as you both age, it can be fun to plan to get your knee replacement surgeries at the same time.

When Your Adorable Brings You Along

Unlike a soccer mom relegated to the sidelines, being a sport with your sporty Adorable is not simply a spectator activity. Even if the event is focused on the dog's performance you will have a role too.

Ten ways to support your sporty Adorable:

- Drying off after a dock dive

- Picking up waste

- Carrying loot

- Caddying and helping calculate shot distances and club choice

- Looking sporty and giving direction to the agility champ (no bow ties and tweed in this Westminster competition)

- Carrying equipment

- Telling your Adorable to "stick and move." And warning them when to avoid an uppercut

- Holding the water bottle

- Waiting on the sidelines with a silk robe

- Building their confidence that the fiery hoops on the course in front of them don't put out much "real heat"

(Maybe it is not so different than a soccer mom after all)

SUPER SPORTY DOGS OF NOTE

These amazing, sporty dogs are at the top of their game and seem to have that innate athleticism typically only seen in the likes of Tiger Woods, LeBron James, and other mega-sporty types.

SPITFIRE (SPITTY)–FIVE-TIME DOCK DIVING CHAMP

Spitty can jump really, really far from a dock, farther than all of the other dogs in the world. His incredible skill has landed him and his charge, 13-year-old Sydney Mackey, five world dock diving records—and counting. To win, Spitty will run down a dock and jump the length of a short bus, and, still airborne after more than 22 feet, grab a chew toy that hangs suspended a few feet above the water, before splashing into the pool. His talents are not limited to the horizontal plane. Like most spectacular athletes he is multifaceted; he also can jump high—high enough to claim a chew toy waved above Steph Curry's head.

This powerful whippet maintained with acupuncture, chiropractic, and a serious training regimen performs spectacular bellyflops and travels far and wide to some of the 1,000 dock diving competitions held in the US each year, where Adorables show off their skill and see if they can get those bellyflops to pay off with some serious prize money. That's right, there are nearly three dock diving competitions per day in the US and they are somehow all accessible by the same competitors. Strangely, the US has only 803 actual docks. @teamsydfire

PINK–MASTER AGILITY DOG, WESTMINSTER DOG SHOW 2020

Pink is as alert as an air traffic controller at SFO and far more athletic. Agility requires dogs to quickly navigate a series of obstacles as their owners run alongside them, giving direction and encouragement. They must go over jumps, through poles, up ramps, and through tunnels faster than all the other highly trained dogs while not incurring any of the long list of infractions like dropped bars, skipped obstacles, and even entering the weave poles from the right rather than the left. Pink did all of this with the quick direction of her handler but also instinctively reads the flow of the course. She recognizes patterns at a dead sprint, chooses the logical route whenever it exists, and takes obvious pleasure in picking correctly, which led to her multiple wins at Westminster and becoming 2020 Master Agility winner. Pink's handler has three children that come to each event and are completely out of control. Strangely, this doesn't count against their points total at all. @pinkthebc

FISSION—WORD'S FASTEST FLYBALLER 2020

As noted by the 2020 flyball rankings, flyball is one of the more inclusive sports—the extensive rule book notes that the sport is open to all breeds. Perfect for Fission, a mixed breed flyballer, indeed the fastest of 2020. He and his teammates love balls, are trained to have recall, and are as fit and healthy as any sprinter. On a typical day of flyball the noise is loud. Handler Tori Stewart strains to hold Fission at the start line. The blue light changes to yellow, to green. Fission takes off. She races to the first hurdle and clears it. To the second hurdle. The third. The fourth. She hits the box with her front foot. Boom! A tennis ball flies out. Fission swiftly snaps it up, turns around, and clears each hurdle once again. She crosses the finish line passing nose to nose with her teammate in seconds. This incredible speed propelled her to the top of the 2020 leaderboard. Flyball is not allowed to be played around men who are coming out of the shower.

ALICE—FORMER DOG DANCING WORLD CHAMPION

If you weren't the kid sitting in a corner at childhood ballet classes and instead are the one to get up dancing before you've had two cocktails, dog dancing may be the outlet you and your Adorable are looking for. Alice, the dog that two-steps better than your Kentucky cousin, and her charge have over 3.1m views on YouTube on just one of their routines, making dog dancing a serious opportunity to get the search engine algorithm working in your favor. Alice is keyed into her dance partner and there is no stepping on toes here as she puts *Dancing with the Stars* contestants to shame. The two have obviously spent multiple hours, days, months, and years working to move in perfect synergy but Alice steals the show. Choreography is important since dancers also dress up according to the theme of the dance, so *These Boots Are Made for Walking* may be a tough sell.

LEVI—TREIBBALL ENTHUSIAST

Levi once lived with a family that had to give him up because he became too protective, scaring guests and visitors. The Sanctuary, Levi's rescue organization, gave him a much more constructive "project" to work on and helped bring out his best behavior. If your Adorable has pushed your exercise ball back after it went rogue, you have a natural on your hands, like Levi. Treibball, German for "drive ball," or more loosely translated, "ball herding," has been found to develop focus, confidence, and impulse control in dogs. At the competition, eight exercise balls are arranged in a triangle at center field. Depending on the age and size division of the dog, the canines have seven to 10 minutes—dogs seven years and up get an extra two minutes—to "herd" them toward their handler and into a goal. Unfortunately, this means your Adorable can never go with you to a workout class at your local rec center. Not only will all the balls in the building be stolen and pushed through a doorway, so will any roundish-shaped person.

THE SPORTY METER

How sporty are you and your pal? Being Adorables, limitations in life are few and far between, however, a sportiness factor is important and does require some attention if it's lacking. Before you head out to be a @loki check in on your sportiness level, which usually equates to the social media follower count that will result from the sportiness.

THE SPORTY METER

Use to assess sportiness, and to determine whether to spectate or participate

If you land on the Not Sporty side you may still be able to participate with human assistance

Owns a lite jacket

Owns a doggie backpack and booties

Has paddle boarded without jumping off

Plays some form of fetch daily

Knows how to skateboard

Has a basket or trailer for bike

Surfs Solo

Makes indent in couch so that all housemates observe dedicated couch position

Knows how to mush

Routinely paraglides

Not Sporty

Super Sporty

Dear Kendra,

I recently adopted the most adorable and lovable retired greyhound. I have loved greyhounds for years and find them incredibly stoic and proud. I was told that this particular greyhound, aptly named EatMhyDst retired from racing due to a sore knee. He has fully recovered and now all he wants to do is run, really fast! Did you know greyhounds can run 45 miles an hour? I am not a runner and I prefer short walks on long beaches. What can I do?

—Unsportiest

Dear Unsportiest,

Have you ever been to a field off leash park or a dog friendly beach and noticed that all dogs consistently travel over 400 times father than their charges? All relationships take compromise. Yours will be to get your greyhound out and about in an off-leash area so he can go 45 miles an hour without you in tow. No true sportiness is required, and you can watch all of this from a comfortable vantage point. Your only consideration will be to keep the smallest of children, rabbits (the cue to run in his former life) and Pekingese (which can be mistaken as rabbits) out of his way.

You got this!

PS Don't forget the slowmo mode on your camera or to attach a GoPro which can attach to his harness as both options make for excellent footage.

Kendra

CHAPTER 16

DATING WITH DOGS: NAVIGATING FIRST PUP DATES, DEAL BREAKERS, AND NEW PARTNERS

Dating is affected by Adorables, as is much of the rest of life. There are certain conventions that make the dating dance with an Adorable as complex and fraught with traps as a game of chess with your cheating father-in-law.

In the end, what everyone wants is a true mate, but while some are not sure if they want a third (and furry) party in the relationship, others may bond more with your Adorable than you. Yet others may be similarly equipped with their own, which either also barks or, to further complicate things, meows. Either way getting to the next step can require steering clear of some landmines (not the dog doo ones) that if not navigated correctly may deter you from finding the love of your life and instead create a sworn enemy.

MEETING PROSPECTS

Whether at a dog park or walking through an outdoor mall your attractiveness and approachability quadruples knowing just this one word: puppy. The puffier (or flouffier, in dog lexicon) the puppy the better. Men will approach you; women will approach you, and extraterrestrials will approach you to see and pet your puppy. It's called "puppy gravity" and there is no escape. Note: you should not get a puppy for this reason alone. An Adorable is a real long-term commitment, unlike anything you can have with another person.

If you can get into the best shape of your life, you can maximize your puppy gravity.

Dog Park. Dogs do all the work at this hangout making it easy to move on to first-date-level conversations. Be wary of those who have borrowed a dog for this exact purpose and what that may reveal. Anyone who doesn't share a home with an Adorable may get "A" for effort but in the end they're like a keto donut—too far from the real thing to be enjoyable.

Blind Date. A handy way to meet someone, as any friend close enough to introduce you to a possible lifetime mate will

HOW TO MAKE AN ONLINE DATING PROFILE

1. Gather Tools

Favorite pictures (you and Harry look particularly photogenic), photographer (may require feeding or pay), camera, dog, phone

2. Google Yourself

What will they see - if you have pictures of keg stands in college no matter what your profile says you may not get a wink unless they are still in that phase of their life.

3. Get Creative Juices Flowing

Think of the profile of your ideal mate, write it, and then edit for truthfulness. Get Inspo from others, then Google "How to make a great dating profile."

4. Pick Your Site

The more niche the better the odds - think canine dating online as opposed to bikerplanet.com unless you have a dedicated sidecar.

5. Pick a Username

This is not your passcode - everyone will see it! Also a great time to reveal how creative and amazing you are. Choose Fithiker as opposed to Looseygoosey or Iluvmabel

6. Write Your Profile

Be honest, the jig is up if you stretch the truth too far which is more likely to lead to an enemy than the opposite. "Share home with an adorable well behaved shih tzu" as opposed to "Live solo and my car and home are free of dog hair."

7. Add Pictures.

Add pictures. Not pictures from 10 years ago but recent pictures that are airbrushed and preferably include one with your Adorable on the beach or doing something active and fun.

8. Stop.

Review. Funny but not too funny? Honest but not too honest? But what are you missing? Add some and Review Again. Maybe swap out a picture and keep repeating until it is just right. Put it online and see if you're attracting your targeted group. Once you have nailed it, show it to a friend - did they recognize it was your profile? If not, start at step one.

also be keenly aware of your Adorable and his role in your life.

The downside to blind dates is that your friends may set you up with someone who makes you realize that "these people aren't really friends."

If they really are your friends after all, it will save you from exerting a ridiculous amount of brain power letting your significant other know that they will always be number two in your life. But that's a really good place to be. (You will also need to find out if they are willing to pick up a lot of number "two.")

Online Dating. Thirty percent of all US adults have used online dating, 48 percent of whom are between 18 and 29 years old. Online dating allows you to throw the net wider than ever. Last year alone the number of long-term relationships in the US that began with online dating was .0001 percent. If you have a picture of you holding a cat the number is zero.

Online Dating Profile. Opinions abound as to what should be included in a profile. Its only purpose is to lead your ideal partner to immediately recognize there is a match with you. But you are a special breed, as is your Adorable, and therefore need to have them recognize that any match will include your most significant partner.

SUCCESSFUL COMPATABILITY SPECTRUM

They hate dogs

They know people with dogs and think they are cute

SWEET

OKAY

A five-month-old photo of you and your Adorable

Using an alias

Listing your favorite quotes, one of which is something like, "A true friend leaves paw prints on your heart"

Mentioning that your dog is really special

Showing a picture of you and your pet chilling

Having an accurate relationship status

Saying you would like to train your dog to do some funny tricks

Wearing red in your profile pic*

According to multiple research studies, both men and women rate members of the opposite sex wearing something red as more attractive.

Goal = find companion in the sweet spot

SPOT

They are a dog musher and Have 20 dogs

They own a Dog boarding facility

Loves dogs, always wanted One

NOT OKAY

Multiple five-year-old photos of you and your Adorable

Impersonating a much cooler person than yourself

Listing multiple quotes all regarding the loyalty of a dog and pretending you said them

Itemizing all your dog's attributes and awards

Showing you and your Adorable in your PJs enjoying breakfast in bed

Saying you are in a relationship with your dog. You are, but you can't say it out loud (or in your profile).

Saying that you have quit your job and recently moved to Hollywood to focus on your Adorable's budding modeling and movie career (plus including you have A LOT of spare time of late)

Using your dog as your profile picture or a close up of you and your dog*

*Research indicates that photos taken with people less attractive than you make you automatically look hotter. It's called the "Ugly Friend Effect," and it instantly makes you look better online, which means the opposite is also true if your far cuter Adorable is included in your profile picture.

Dear Kendra,

A couple of months ago I met my girlfriend on compatible-doglover.com. She assumed I shared my life with a dog, and I did not correct her. I have had a dog on my vision board for 20 years but by talking to my girlfriend he came alive. I ended up describing my vision board dog on our dates in great detail. I even named him Masha, after my favorite cartoon Masha and the Bear, and applied a breed and origin story to my vision board dog, a boxer/lab cross that I rescued from a kill shelter while on a mission in Tennessee. I am afraid that if I tell her the truth, she will dump me. What do I do?

I need your help.
Voracious Vision Boarder aka Tall Tales Ted

....

Dear Voracious Vision Boarder,

You'd better start hightailing it to all the shelters in the US and online to find this vision board replica. Some would say to come clean, but this is a calling, man—your vision board worked! On the other hand, telling her you never meant to deceive her but instead got caught up in the excitement will only doubly disappoint; first that you are a liar, since you did mean to deceive her with your fake profile pic, and second, she'll be bummed out that she won't get to have Adorable double dates and hear your Adorable speak with a Southern accent. In the interim get some dog accessories and place them around the house in case she comes over and you have not yet found him. You can say that he is at your parents' for a visit since they are crazy about their granddoggie and you feel compelled to share his adorableness and his cute southern drawl with others.

The other option is just at the right moment call her up, sobbing, and break the horrible news that Masha is gone. Don't say dead. Just say every sentence that might include dead and replace it with "gone." You won't be lying, and she will love you even more. This is a good time to see how she reacts in a crisis and if she doesn't try to make you feel better over your dead" "no-longer-with-you" dog, dump the insensitive b∰%#@.

Good Luck!
—Kendra

TOP DATING DILEMMAS

You're having a great time and then your date says something offensive about pets and the people that share their households with them.

First step is always to confirm. Ask them to clarify the statement, "Dogs are stupid and so are their owners." When they proceed on a long diatribe about a roommate and how they slept with their disgusting dog and how it pees all over and steals their things, calmly ask if their sole judgement on dogs is based on this one experience and if a well-trained dog would change their mind. If they consider the question thoughtfully, there may be hope and you can keep going. If they refuse to view the alternative perception with an open mind insist that your mom is calling and jet. If you're feeling particularly feisty and you have some privacy, lift your leg on their things.

YOUR DATE DOES NOT KNOW ABOUT YOUR ADORABLE. WHEN IS THE BEST TIME TO SHARE?

Unless you met at the dog park or online (with an honest dating profile) your date may not be aware of your Adorable and all his glory. The sooner you get it out, the better. Your Adorable will surely have a positive impact and will be entered on the side of the paper labelled "Pros." That means their reaction to him will enter the "Pros" column on your list as well. Have your date pick you up at your house and be ready when he arrives with your Adorable beside you at the door or in your arms. This maneuver will help break the news gently. If your Adorable is still sniffing crotches then maybe sharing some well-curated Adorable iPhone photos into your second glass of wine would be better.

If you just tell your date that you have an Adorable who means the world to you, listen for the tonal sound of the response not the words. If they say, "Ohhh," with connotations of, "Mmmm," as in, "This is tasty," then you're in luck; they love dogs.

If the pitch of the "Ohhh" sounds like the start of a Michael Jackson song, it's bad news and you should try to make them pay the bill.

YOUR ADORABLE APPEARS TO LIKE YOUR DATE MORE THAN YOU

This can be upsetting, but do not forget you are the one cuddling with your Adorable each night; you take him out to pee at 2 a.m.; you take him to the beach and out for ice cream. From your Adorable's perspective, another person in the relationship is a positive: it's an extra person to shower him with love. Warning: make sure your date is not sneaking him treats to win your affection. Cheaters cheat.

YOU AGREE TO A SECOND DATE EVEN THOUGH THEY PREVIOUSLY ADMITTED THEY DO NOT LIKE DOGS

Optimists among Adorable-lovers may think they can change their prospective mate, and given your Adorable's adorableness there is a high likelihood of that. However, even so this will be a lifelong issue. Picture the stink-eye every time your dog gets more attention than they do or destroys the neatly made bed Best to cut this off now—see real Reddit thread below, reflecting this prediction. Although you agreed to a second date you didn't say when and attention spans are so short, you'll be forgotten in no time.

TRUE TAIL: REDDIT THREAD
It's really hard to date someone with a dog

Having a dog is like having a kid. People can never meet up for drinks after work, because they always have to get home to take the dog out. Dinner? Sure! Wait, why are you wolfing it down and asking for the che— Oh, right...the dog.

I met this girl last week that I'm really into, but she has this giant-ass mastiff/pitbull that fetches its slobbery ball and drops it in your lap and whines until you throw it again. My house is full of cashmere and silk and walnut and crystal, and this girl keeps bugging me to let her bring her dog over. I keep gingerly dropping hints that I don't want that, because I kind of do like her, but I feel like this is ultimately going to be a deal-breaker. I just do not want dogs in my house. She's so certain that her dog is the most special, well-behaved dog in the world (even had it trained as a service dog!). Don't care. Still a dog. I like nice things. Oh, he can just sleep on the floor! Okay, what about my carpet? And what about when he inevitably gets bored and antsy?

I'm going to end up just telling her a flat no, and she's going to get offended and feel like I'm calling her a bad dog mom, or suggesting her dog is a particularly smelly beast, and that's going to be the last I see of her. Oh well. At least there won't be a dog in my house.

YOU NEED TO CALL IT OFF, BUT YOUR DOGS BECAME GREAT FRIENDS

Sometimes the chemistry only happens between the Adorables. If you can stand their company mention the lack of chemistry between you both and say that you would still like to meet at the dog park. If they, like you, place their Adorable's needs high on the list then they will rise above a failed romance so that their Adorable can have fun. If you just can't bear to hang around with your ex, no worries—dogs have no sense of time so they don't know if they haven't seen their buddy for five minutes or five years. Either way, get rid of all photos of your ex and his buddy.

Deal-Breakers

You decided it was time to introduce your new prospect to your Adorable with a walk in the park to gauge compatibility. Knowing when a relationship's not working and ending it is hard, but the following scenarios all make it easier.

- Your Adorable jumped up and snagged a cashmere sweater that was met with a screech and a demand for dry cleaning and repairs.

- Your Adorable dropped his ball at their feet, but they did not even notice and appeared to be immune from his charm and irresistibility.

- Your Adorable wiped his face or shook drool that rained down on your date and was met with high drama and a return home for a shower.

- Asked, "Does that dog ever shut up?" after your Adorable , tearing it up with his friends, barked non-stop at the dog park.

- Suggested that you attend some dog obedience classes after your Adorable stopped for a few sniffs on the way to the park.

- Did not appear to even notice that your Adorable was with you.

- Talked incessantly about their cat and mentioned that once she was leash-trained she could come along.

- Marveled at how good looking the other dogs were but did not mention your Adorable's adorableness.

- Threw a ball to your Adorable in very risky locations: over the hill, under bushes, into traffic.

What They Say vs. What They Really Mean:

They say: Are you sure he needs to go out again?
They mean: Why does that dog have to wreck the moment every time?

They say: I…um…love dogs.
They mean: I will tolerate dogs because I like you.

They say: Do you smell that?
They mean: Good God, was that you? Is there anything I should know? Or, I just farted; thank God you have a dog to blame.

They say: Do you really let him do that?
They mean: You spoil your dog. Your children will be nightmares.

They say: Doesn't he have his own bed?
They mean: I am really sick of this dog sleeping in between us.

They say: I…um…love you.
They mean: I will tolerate you, because I like sex.

THE NEXT STEP–MOVING IN

The Big Choice—Your Final Options

You think your dating life is coming to an end and there are just two final contenders to choose between. Normally simply the high drama moment on reality TV dating shows (but you never know). Choosing the right mate is imperative to not having discord in the future when you may yearn for dogs numbers two and three.…

Throughout your dating life you will have naturally listened for cues that reveal your partner's true position on dogs. Certain stories about childhood are particularly revealing, such as this one: the story of how the family childhood dog had to live outside and when your date requested a warm bed for his dog, his mother threw a piece of newspaper out the front door onto the cement steps.

In the example below, this roommate of an Adorable has found two prospects who are in love with her. Both have dazzling résumés, but can you tell which is the-less-than-perfect choice?

	KEENAN	KORIN
Background	Delivered in a home water birth with dogs having the odd drink from the birthing pool.	Born in the hospital. The dogs were relegated to be "outside dogs" as soon as the baby was brought home from the hospital.
Hobby	Hiking	Hockey, Motorcross
Favorite Movie	Tie between *Old Yeller* and *Togo* (depending on mood)	*The Bourne Identity* or *Fast & Furious*
Last Book Read	*The Call of the Wild* by Jack Kerouac	*Green Eggs and Ham*, read to niece
Phone Home Screen	A picture of you and your dog	A picture of with buddies at a recent bachelor(ette) party
Parents' Position on Dogs	Mother keenly wears hat that says "Dog Grandma" to sister's Labrador retriever. Dad happily takes your dog for walks when they visit.	When visiting they frequently request the lint roller and roll their eyes with impatience when you need to get in a quick walk with your Adorable before heading out for the evening. Also, they mumble, "Oh, God, it touched me."
Dog Memory Challenge Game	Can name his pets alphabetically forward and backwards.	What was her name again, Samantha? No, Duke?

As you can tell, Keenan is the outright winner for reasons that are not so subtle. Keenan will clearly be used to the idea that dogs are an integral part of life having had long-term exposure to a lot of fur, drool, and inconvenience related to the family dogs' needs.

This will make it easier to adapt to the minor inconveniences that you and your dog will most certainly bring into their life. Favorite books and movies are also revealing. The fact that your pet is included on the phone home screen shows that you are already linked as a package in their mind.

Finally, parents-in-law. The transition to additional family members is hard enough. Certain traits of you and your parents will be chastised, so it's important that your love of dogs is not added to the list.

Let's take the true tail of a parent-in-law who attempts to avoid petting a Great Dane (near impossible). When the inevitable brief touch occurs, she asks to wash her hands immediately to avoid soiling her steering wheel. Now, such as person just may not set the necessary dog-loving example to her child and will likely be critical of all things dog moving forward.

Dating with dogs can be complicated but when you find the right match the love in your household will be magnified a thousand times over and the amount of "presents" you pick up in the backyard will be cut in half. That's a good reason to settle for Mr. or Mrs. Right Now, not Mr. or Mrs. Right.

CHAPTER 17

DOGSMAID:
INCORPORATING A DOG INTO A WEDDING

Given the Adorable's status within the family there comes a time when being part of a wedding celebration is an inevitable event. It's never a matter of, "Is it appropriate for him?" The answer is always, "Yes." Harry should be included, and a lot. Those that share their home with an Adorable will begin by considering all roles and participants of the ceremony with great care and consideration. They will immediately realize that there is no family member or friend that ranks higher than their Adorable. He simply must be part of the soon-to-be succession of events known as The Wedding. This is an opportunity to love, see love, and be loved.

The Engagement Announcement or Wedsite. The announcement, once traditionally seen in a newspaper, serves to announce to the world the soon-to-be wedded coupling bliss along with insight into the couple's lives and their lineage. Nowadays, the announcement is more likely to be in the form of a wedsite, paired with an announcement on social media.

@threeisnotacrowd · FOLLOW · ···

All you need is LOVE! We are getting married best proposal ever! Harry delivered the ring!

The wedsite includes a welcome message, an "About Us" page, and the bridal party bios, among other sections.

The Wedsite provides ample opportunity to introduce your Adorable, highlight his role in your love story, and profess your ongoing commitment to him (as if anyone invited to the wedding would doubt it, but just in case your soon-to-be significant other's third cousin might). It can be a great way to add to your Adorable's community by posting and referencing the great event. People will be more interested in seeing your Adorable's photos and hearing his stories than hearing about the nuptials. If you want your ceremony to garner any chatter, then your Adorable is the correct starting place. There will be polite but minimal interest in hearing vows or seeing family dancing photos, but a photo of your Adorable who just caught the bouquet...priceless.

Wedsite curation takes a certain skill in that it needs to portray valuable information and express your excitement of the big day at the same time. Your intro is important as it will be the first touchpoint to your audience. If you need assistance here is an example:

Fred, Amber, and Harry are getting hitched!

Welcome to our wedding website. We can't wait to celebrate our special day with you!

We've created this website as a convenient and interactive way to spread the news about all the important details in the lead up to our wedding and to share our triad love story.

You can also get to know Harry, our baby that we had out of wedlock. Scandal! He helped bring us together and will be part of our awesome bridal party (as a ringbearer.) Check out our registry information (don't forget Harry—we have selected some items for him too!).

So have fun, take a look around, and don't forget to RSVP!

Finally, thank you for your ongoing love and support and for welcoming Harry into your lives as one of us. We are so excited to share this day with you all. We look forward to dancing the night away with all of our favorite people—and following Harry as he leads the conga line!

PLANNING THE WEDDING PARTY

As you start to pair the dizzying roles and responsibilities of a wedding party to your closest friends and family members, your Adorable's assignment should be decided first: ring bearer, best man, flower girl? Flower girl and boy would be apt—this role was traditionally meant to encourage procreation with flowers and spices. How fitting! Your Adorable already did contribute to your loving bond!

Don't worry about offending anyone; your family members know that their nieces and nephews, although cute, are not as cute as your Adorable. And if Aunt Nancy is pissed that her children are not serving as ring bearer/ flower girls and have been replaced with a dog, offer them other positions like DJ or cast members to your Adorable's walk down the aisle. After all, throwing flower petals may be a bit distracting to him and will be challenging enough without opposable thumbs. There are many perfect support roles for the disgruntled.

Standard practice is to settle on the role of ring bearer for your Adorable. The job is a two-parter: the first is to carry the wedding rings on a pillow to the altar; the second is to look ridiculously cute while doing it. (After research revealed that this ceremonial function is usually done with fake rings the pressure is off to brush up on the "come" command.)

Alternatively, consider the role of best man for your Adorable as this position is responsible for supporting the groom through the entire planning process and on the big day itself. Your Adorable would beat old college roommates and brothers-in-law on the support scale and would not contribute to social awkwardness by sleeping with the bridesmaids (and if he did it would only be in the most platonic way).

Clothing. Nowhere is wedding convention more strictly observed than clothing selections with the dual goal of following tradition and not showing up the bride. Your Adorable already may do that just because of who he is. Like a mother-in-law who insists on wearing white, gearing up your Adorable in a superhero costume, named "Super Wedding Puppy" is not appropriate.

Although your Adorable is normally the one in the spotlight, get used to the idea that on this occasion, his should be one of a supporting role. Rest assured that his natural adorableness will carry him through. There are a ton of Adorable accessory options: a simple bow tie, vest, flower-adorned cute collar, or bandana will do without going over the top with full-on wedding garb. If you have taught him how to walk on his hind legs don't request this maneuver during the wedding. Oh sure, it would be cute to see him in a tiny tux walking down the aisle with the ring, but that's all anyone will be talking about.

Multiple Festivities. As the wedding draws near you will be busy writing a $1,000 check to everyone you meet. Your schedule will be crowded, and you'll need to determine which festivities your Adorable will attend. There will be showers, bachelor and bachelorette parties, brunches, the wedding rehearsal, and of course the big day itself. There is so much to do at a wedding and so much can go wrong, besides the marriage. This, coupled with the added pressure and obscene importance placed on this day, ensures that any misstep by an Adorable will get blown out of proportion.

Note: the more time on the festivity circuit the higher the odds of disaster. The bride and groom get off easy. All they have to do is show up and act polite and follow on with some thank yous, whereas your Adorable will have to remember not go to the bathroom in awkward places and stave off the desire to partake in all the tasty food offerings just out of reach. At least when anyone is watching.

Top Reported Wedding No-Nos by Furry Wedding Participants

Your Adorable with the ring, your Adorable on the dance floor. Precious images of your dog's participation in your wedding celebrations will surely abound. The reality, however, is that your dog can rehearse his role in the ceremony, but you are not home free even if he learns the mandated walk down the aisle and ring hand off.

Reported wedding no nos include:

- Stealing a high heel from a bridesmaid
- Peeing on the altar
- Barking during the first toast
- Scratching himself with large thumps during the nuptials
- Licking himself—and then the cake
- Tripping the bride
- Biting the father of the bride as he presents his daughter
- Running off with the ring (for a swim or otherwise)
- Eating the ring
- Rubbing his butt down the aisle
- Jumping on the child guests and leaving pawprints
- Barking through all the toasts
- Disappearing, warranting an 18-hour search
- Growling at the officiant
- Breaking the photographer's camera
- Inappropriately sniffing the entire wedding party one at a time
- Knocking down a centenarian
- Barking at a screaming centenarian
- Using unnecessary roughness to catch the bouquet

The Nuptials and Ceremony. Except in large cities, over 80 percent of nuptials or ceremonies are near water, lakes, oceans, and rivers. After the guests arrive, they may chill out with a cocktail. Here your Adorable can appropriately mingle. Guests will then move to their seats with a view of the body of water framed by an altar decorated in themed colors. If your Adorable is one to enjoy floating objects in bodies of water, ensure that he is managed during this time and does not swim off with the rings. You can buy change-of-heart insurance in the event the entire thing is called off, but your insurance company may dispute a coverage claim based on an unruly or absent pet.

WEDDING PARTICIPATION OPTIONS
for your ADORABLE
☑ Greeting guests...
☒ Passing around hors d'oeuvres
☒ You may now kiss the bride
☑ Bouquet catch...
☒ Pulling off the garter
☑ Smashing cake in his face
☑ Dance with father of the bride
☑ Macarena
☑ Ride to the hotel
☒ The wedding night
☑ Honeymoon

Amazing photo ops aside, the celebratory wedding exit is a feature that dates back to Roman times. Showering the newlyweds with rice as they exit their ceremony or reception has been a wedding tradition for a long, long time and is considered a symbol of prosperity, good fortune, and fertility, and the perfect way to usher them into their new life together.

However, rice may not be the best idea with any Adorables that are the vacuum sort. Your frantic Adorable knocking over Granny to get to the auspicious grain is not ideal. This does not mean you should give up on the photo op of an exit as there are many other items your guests can toss (or ring or wave!) to send you off on your wedding night: sparklers, bubbles,

HOW TO FEATURE YOUR ADORABLE THROUGHOUT THE FESTIVITIES (NOT JUST IRL)

Due to the huge amount of printable matter required prior to and at weddings themselves there are a myriad of opportunities for your dog to show up in a watercolor image, silhouette, or embossed image or pawprint. The following are some of the most popular:

- Invitation for any and all festivities

- Directional signs

- Bar signs (perhaps a signature drink–think Harry's G&T with cucumber shaves)

- Glassware

- Goodie bags

- Napkins

- Just Married sign

- Exit flags

- Bathroom signs (Dawgs, Bitches)

- Cake decoration (Man/Wife/ Adorable)

- Table centerpiece

flags, Snausages, and lavender all provide good photo opportunities.

@threeisnotacrowd FOLLOW ...

We did it. "Just Married!" The doves survived.

THE HONEYMOON

As in many other aspects of your lives, you may decide to incorporate your Adorable into your honeymoon plans—usually, to somewhere tropical or warm. There are many honeymoon options, such as hiking or camping excursions, where your Adorable can be easily included.

Driving off from the wedding in a classic car with your dog's mournful eyes gazing after you amongst the cheering crowd will be incredibly sad (provided he returns from chasing the doves). Your departure will almost certainly be construed by your Adorable as punishment and particularly unfair after all his good behavior. Even if building sandcastles with your Adorable on an extended tropical vacation is not in the plan, including him initially may be a good idea.

THE CHECKLIST

PHOTOGRAPHY - GIFTS - DECORATIONS - BEAUTY - BUDGETS

What They Would Have Done Differently

100 recent brides reveal their wedding missteps

WHAT DO YOU REGRET SPLURGING ON?

Hair & Makeup 55%
Harry's Custom - Tailored Tuxedo 0%
Drinks 0%
Dress 90%
Fees for Harry to Join Honeymoon 2%
Harry's Custom Logo and
Printing on Invites and Decorations 1%
Everything Else 83%

WHAT DID YOU DO WITH YOUR DRESS?

Properly Stowed it
6%
Still at Cleaner's for Stain Removal of Muddy Paw Prints
75%
Other
15%
Repurposed it
4%

WHAT WAS YOUR BEST GIFT?

1. Vacuum Cleaner
2. Custom Couch Cover

WHAT WAS YOUR BRIDEZILLA MOMENT?

"I yelled at my maid of honor for not respecting my dog."

"I made the tailor do three fittings of of my dog's tuxedo."

"The photographer wanted some pictures without my dog in them and I refused and yelled at her."

CAN YOU STILL DEFEND IT?

Yes . . . 99%
No 1%

WHAT PART OF YOUR WEDDING WAS THE MOST MEMORABLE?

"Jumping into the lake with my dog and my new husband!"
"Seeing my dog appear with the rings and bringing them right to us."
"Getting in the horse drawn carriage after the reception and seeing my dog propped up next to the carriage driver."

WHAT DO YOU WISH YOU HAD PAID MORE/LESS ATTENTION TO?

More	*Less*
"Spending time with Harry instead of parents and coworkers."	"Going to the park with Harry rather than obedience classes."
"Attending obedience classes with Harry."	"Seating charts."
"Teaching Harry how to do the 'electric slide.'"	"Concern over whether people like dogs."

WHAT MEMORIES MAKE YOU CRINGE?

"My dog shaking and drenching several guests after a lake swim"
"Cutting a cake with a large bite out of it"
"The muddy paw prints on my dress, especially during the first dance"
"Harry taking a bathroom break at the altar"

WHAT DO YOU WISH YOU HAD SPENT MORE ON?

Dance lessons for Harry . . . .86%   A higher table for the cake . . 78%   Stain-proofing my dress 92%
Dance lessons for myself . . . 16%   A more secure collar. . . . . . .15%   Chew toys 68%

A True Cautionary Tail: Dog Required

A couple of years ago, the daughter of a close friend of mine was getting married. She took on her duties with zeal, one of which was to ensure that her French bulldog, a classic Adorable, was at the wedding to perform his well-practiced and endearing duty of ring bearer. The scene was set, the guests began to arrive, the anticipation was rising as the pre-wedding buzz resonated through the attendees. The wedding was huge with over 300 guests on a remote ranch. All were present except the ring bearer. Gus had been primed, prepped, and rehearsed but during all the packing up and checklists the little star had been completely forgotten and left behind at the bride-to-be's house. Home Alone: Gus's Story. Upon realizing his absence, my friend's heart sank and panic set in. Too remote for an Uber, her mind was spinning.

A suggestion from one guest was a luxury option and $500 later Gus arrived in his own black luxury SUV, flashing lit floorboards, minibar, and all. Gus missed the nuptials (he was replaced by a less adorable child option) and his absence was felt by all with a palliative gloom over the guests and anxious guilt in the mother of the bride. He was there for the rest of the festivities and was able to dance and partake in the toast. Gus is still remembered as being a hit of the party with an overhang that is paired with wistful feelings of regret for missing his moment in the limelight with the bride and groom.

Weddings are full of competing demands. If you choose to include your best friend, make sure he makes it to the altar.

CHAPTER 18

THE ADORABLE AUTOMOBILE: SELECTING THE PERFECT CAR

"Is this love?"

This is what my friend thought as he gazed across the parking lot and first saw a heel, then a white pant leg slide out of the vehicle, followed by four furry legs that nimbly dropped to the ground. Once out of the vehicle, the Adorable alternated between gazing up at her tall owner and facing into the weather to achieve that wind-blown look. My friend knew intuitively knew he was in love.

Not love like he wanted to propose but the love that comes with the full appreciation of unconditional love of a dog that comes out of a high-end vehicle.

It all started with the vehicle.

This combination of canine and car caused him to sprint down to the

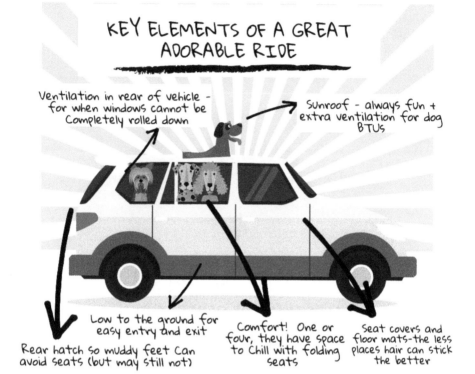

KEY ELEMENTS OF A GREAT ADORABLE RIDE

Ventilation in rear of vehicle - for when windows cannot be completely rolled down

Sunroof - always fun + extra ventilation for dog BTUs

Low to the ground for easy entry and exit

Rear hatch so muddy feet can avoid seats (but may still not)

Comfort! One or four, they have space to chill with folding seats

Seat covers and floor mats-the less places hair can stick the better

Land Rover dealer and immediately procure one for his daughter. He then dashed to a local breeder who specialized in doggy-to-driver matching. He wanted his daughter to garner similar admiration from others and this same feeling has driven the car buying decision for millions of others since.

Your Adorable deserves the same level of adoration when she exits her ride. Your vehicle selection may provide it since what you drive is an essential tool and a critical element of style and adoration. This is as important for any dog as choosing the correct collar/leash combination.

You may think that you do not intend to take your dog anywhere. You are making a huge mistake.

Going out and about is not only necessary, but a major opportunity for stardom. The vet, dog park, trailhead, and beach are all places you need to go at some point. These could lead to double viral incidents. Not only will you post an Adorable/vehicle image but so does someone else who has fallen in love with your Adorable, your car, and possibly you.

Here are some features you may want to consider. Depending on the size, age, and number of dogs some may be more important than others:

EASY ENTRY AND EXIT

Rear entry. It's really handy when dogs can have their own door to jump in and out of with ease without traipsing dirty paws over your seat. For peak impression, set out a small step so your star doesn't have to jump all the way to the ground (we will leave thoughts of a red carpet to you). Protect those delicate paws from danger.

Or go with…

A low-to-the-ground profile. This is especially important as dogs age. You do not want to be the one lifting a 70-pound wet dog into a car. A low profile makes it easier for dogs of all sizes and ages to climb in and out with fewer scratches to the exterior.

COMFORT

Folding seats. Seats are generally uncomfortable for dogs. You can add seat covers and such but in the end the shape is a bit awkward and unsecure and will inevitably lead to upholstery rips and scratches. Folding seats allow you to easily throw down a dog bed that matches your upholstery and dogs can stretch out solo or with their doggy pal.

KEEPING IT CLEAN

Non-carpeted walls and floors. You may not want or will soon get tired of looking at pesky white hairs in your headliner and carpeting. Although seeing evidence of your pet in the form of hair in the headliner (that dutiful car detailers have been unable to remedy for years after your furry friend has passed) may put a smile on your face. It may be an issue for those who have to ride along with you and will most certainly reduce the resale value of your vehicle. They will likely fear those same headliner hairs will be catching a ride out of the vehicle with them. Less carpeting means fewer places for hairs to stick, and easy cleanup. At a minimum, removable cargo liners and mats are completely necessary so you can take them out and dislodge hair with a good cleaning occasionally.

VENTILATION

For dog pals that have more BTUs than the rest of us, windows in the back that go down are critical—see that iconic image of a dog with its head out the window.

Rear A/C vents that are independently adjusted are equally important so that pals that typically run a bit hotter than you will be equally as comfortable.

Sunroof or moonroof to provide the maximum ventilation without your dog being able to jump (or fall) out.

MAKES AND MODELS

Luckily, many car manufacturers have realized the buying power of Adorables and therefore taken you and your pet's needs into account.

RANGE ROVER, JEEP, TOYOTA 4RUNNER, MERCEDES GLS

These types of vehicles are essential to your lifestyle with the rationale that your yearning for dog adventures will have you on remote private roads and parking lots, like the parking lot at the beach, or staging area for your

@pawsitivleypawsome   FOLLOW   •••

"I love the feeling of the fresh air on my face and the wind blowing in my hair." -Evil Kneivel

next hike. All of these models have features that will withstand sandy, dirty paws, like rugged interiors and great ventilation. Of course, the Range Rover tops the chart. Range Rover execs recognized that over 50 percent of their customers were pet owners, and that the outdoor life of most Range Rover owners includes a dog. The optional pet pack caters to those with dog pals and includes things like an access ramp, portable shower, spill-resistant water bowl, and foldable pet carrier so that you don't have to worry about muddy paws on the seat as those can be taken care of pre-ride home.

SUBARU OUTBACK OR MERCEDES WAGON

This is the quintessential pet car that accommodates people and pets comfortably. Those that do not want their pet in their lap causing near accidents at every turn can employ a cargo net. You may miss that extra lap time with your dog, but cargo nets can keep dogs in the back and out of the way. These wagons can morph into whatever your needs are at the time, either adorned with paddle boards and outdoor play toys or cleaned up for a tail gate. The low ride height makes getting in and out easy for people and pets and the back of most can be inlaid with a removable, rinseable boot tray.

TESLA

Although sedans, like some of the Tesla models, are the most uncomfortable for dogs, their pet-friendly technology is in a class of its own. Tesla claims to have resolved the difficult problem of pets overheating in vehicles with "Dog Mode," a climate-control feature that leaves the car's air conditioning or heater on when owners leave their pets in the car. Then, most importantly, to avoid smashed windows, nasty notes, and even the police, when you exit your Tesla, a message is displayed on a screen on the dash that reads: "My owner will be back soon. Don't worry! The heater [or A/C] is on and it's XX degrees." The temperature stays where you set it for as long as you are away from the car and you get notified on your phone if it does not, so that you can drop all your purchases at once and sprint back to your vehicle. There have been some complaints of the alerts not working but a Tesla owner is likely also one with faith in driverless vehicles so in general they are not risk-averse when it comes to relying on technology to sub for important human undertakings and those complaints will likely be overlooked.

In addition, Tesla offers utility mats for a small extra cost for all vehicles and there is independent climate control in the rear of the vehicles.

TRUCK

You may have driven down the freeway behind a truck with a pet hanging out the back, lips flapping with utter joy, uncaring and unknowing that he could splat on the tarmac at any moment. In most states dogs are required to be tied in the back but it remains unnerving, nevertheless. The worry is the devastating image of your dog's wind-strewn saliva stretching towards the front windshield of a trailing car. If teens or tweens are riding in that vehicle, your comments section will be littered with gross emojis.

Trucks can be handy, especially for the large dog set as dogs can go in the back and the interior never has to be soiled. However, thought should be given to the safety and temperature needs of your pet if you go with this option. Good news is that newer models have made it so that back seats can fold flat and have introduced other dog-friendly features such as easy-clean upholstery.

The Rear bumper. Reveals your love of dogs and more practically puts others on notice of your infatuation with a dog that may be in your blind spot or on your lap and the cause of erratic driving. Typically, in the form of a bumper sticker, "I Love My …" or "Dog is Good," a simple pawprint or "Dog Is My Co-Pilot."

CRAIGSLIST AD
FOR VEHICLE OF A NEW DOG OWNER
FOR SALE—WELL-LOVED VEHICLE. MAKE AN OFFER

Beloved Wagon regretfully for sale, 150,000 miles. Only selling as need a larger vehicle (welcomed a new dog into the family!). Exterior great condition except scratches on passenger door panel and rear hatch area. Upholstery wear exceeds age of vehicle, and some holes and scratches in rear seat area. Chew marks appear on some handles. Some tears and small hairs appear in headliner. When all four windows are open at a speed of greater than 45mph, unseen hairs can swirl. Child-free car from a non-smoker but pungent odor upon turning heat and A/C on.

CHAPTER 19

AN ADORABLE GUIDE
TO SHOWING THE WORLD YOUR ADORABLE

In the world of Adorables some of the best memories and content is created during travel. Now that you have chosen the correct name, set up your profile, and have basic communication and commands down it is time to venture out into the world.

Here are some important points to bear in mind as you set out.

CONFIRM THE INVITATION

Travel, both locally and nationally, is usually sparked by an invitation. An invitation does not automatically mean that it includes a plus one. Sometimes it's difficult to tell whether Harry is included in the festivities.

In general, your Adorable's behavior serves as an indicator of whether he is welcome. If Harry still humps people's legs and pees in the house, odds are the invitation is just for you. On the other hand, they may not be aware of Harry's existence and therefore a failure to expressly include him on an invite may simply be an oversight. They may also have their own pet, allergies, or just not be a fan of dogs (How did you get this friend?).

Regardless, step one is to clarify the invitation details. This can be done in many ways including a visit to a psychic, a phone call to another invitee, or have your significant other call the host's significant other. What you want to avoid is the host having to say no, or saying yes when she really means no-such behavior can only be predicted by knowing her Myers-Briggs Type Indicator.[7] We have included this handy decision tree to assist with avoiding awkward conversations.

TRUE TAIL
Banned Adorable

There is the oft-told story of the woman who repeatedly assumed that her furry pal was invited to dinner parties. Her friends were consistently forced to spend endless amounts of time and energy trying to figure out ways to have the dog left at home so that scenes like humping everyone's leg, stealing food off plates, crapping on the lawn for the kids to inevitably roll in, and chasing the chickens were avoided (all true occurrences from past parties).

So much time was spent working out how to let the woman know that her Adorable was not an invitee that the quality of the food and the anticipatory party vibe suffered. Post-party conversation was also usually spent retelling the stupefying behavior of her furry pal instead of praising the host's perfectly infused cocktail and other efforts. Eventually, they quit

---

7   The Myers-Briggs Type Indicator (MBTI) personality inventory was developed to make the theory of psychological types as described by C. G. Jung understandable and useful in people's lives. The essence of the theory is that much seemingly random variation in a person's behavior is actually quite orderly and consistent, due to basic differences in the ways that individuals prefer to use their perception and judgment. In the end anyone that takes it is a bit startled due to the accurate results.

asking her.

If your otherwise easygoing clan bans you or your Adorable, it may be a good time for some self-reflection.... At the end of that time, you will usually come to the conclusion, "Oh, f&@$ them anyway." You and your Adorable have better things to do with your time.

IS HARRY A TRUE INVITEE?

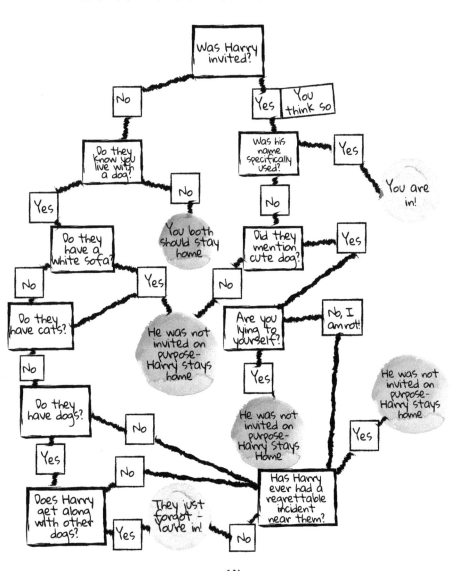

Dear Kendra,

My husband will be having outpatient surgery with almost no risk to his life, but his recovery will be long and painful, with months of physical therapy and many restrictions on what he can do as he recuperates.

His mother wants to assist by being a live-in caregiver.

The biggest problem with having her for a visit is her dog, whom she refers to as her "favorite son." She bought him the most appalling service-dog jacket and forces her way into all non-dog appropriate venues.

I like dogs, as does my husband, but hers is difficult to manage. He is always seemingly over-caffeinated, hyper, aggressive, and a manic digger. He near created an underground tunnel to the local Stop N Save. Barking is as normal and necessary to him as breathing, upholstered furniture is a toilet, and curtains are for climbing. Whenever anyone tells him to stop, including our dog he fights them, having bitten all in our circle at least once—including our pets.

This is all met with zero discipline. Our atrocious houseguest has, to our knowledge, never been reprimanded. We are concerned that the offer to assist is conditioned on my mother-in-law arriving with her dog in tow.

Is there a polite yet firm way to tell her that neither of them may visit? She may be very obtuse about what she is doing to her relationship with her son and grandkids, but she is over-the-top sensitive about feeling rejected herself.

Please help!

—Dogged out Daughter-in-Law

Dear Dogged out Daughter-in-Law,

"We are so grateful for your support. I'm afraid that we are on strict orders to not accept visitor jerks in the form of dog and human while Herman is recovering. If you would like to visit sans puppy pal and not be horrid we will arrange a time for a brief visit."

Notice that while this wording invokes the term "orders" to provide authority, it does not strictly implicate any person in a lie since they are Herman's orders. Still, given your mother-in-law's apparent obstinance, it would not be a bad idea to seek an official-looking mandate.

This ingenious sentence has previously been used with success by myself when I didn't want the following people coming over under similar circumstances: Father Tim and his ex-porn-star-to-converted-nun "assistant"; Aunt Milly and her box of pet toads; and Cousin Rick "The Destroyer" WWE wrestler and his buddy, "The Human Apocalypse." But, honestly, I have never used it in reference to a dog visitor as that is just something I would ever refuse.

With hope,

Kendra

Smells? After sharing your living space with Harry, you may find that at some point your nose gets immune to his various smells, a situation referred to as olfactory fatigue. Also known as odor fatigue, olfactory adaptation, and nose-blindness, this is the temporary, normal inability to distinguish a particular odor after a prolonged exposure to that airborne compound (according to Wikipedia). If you have ever wondered how people can live near a dump, this is likely why. While those folks likely got a great discount on their home for the small sacrifice of living near a dump, olfactory fatigue makes life slightly complicated for the owner of an Adorable who may suffer from the affliction of nose-blindness.

The complication arises if your travels take you to stay amongst those that may not be near an Adorable on a daily basis and therefore do not similarly

suffer from such fatigue. They will have heightened senses and be able to detect any off-putting smell immediately, which can impact first and lasting impressions.

Most importantly, if you are to take your Adorable along on your trip, make sure that he is looking and feeling his best. Do not do anything to cause excessive gas (e.g., changing food or increasing root vegetables in his diet—see Chapter 6) and ensure he has visited his favorite groomer (she also suffers from nose-blindness so do not seek her opinion on his smell level, just have her do a thorough clean).

QUIZ

NAME THE PRODUCT AVAILABLE FOR PURCHASE TO COMBAT PET ODOR

Your Adorable ran through your host's garden and peed on the pumpkins. You leave for home and...

A. Candle Collar. Candles come in dozens of powerful scents normally worse than the smell of a wet dog but only to you. Expert tip: do not light near pet hair.

B. My S&%$ Don't Stank food additive to encourage constipation and produce lavender-scented pellets. Expert tip: Good for weekend trips only or permanent health issues may result.

C. Saran Wrapooch. The convenient protective wrap comes scented and in wider strips to "wrap away that nasty smell." Expert tip: when you return from the trip remove the wrap outdoors as the repressed odor release can cause a massive brain hemorrhage.

D. Rocco & Roxie Supply Professional Strength Stain and Odor Eliminator, Enzyme-Powered Pet Odor and Stain Remover. Expert tip: Not for direct application to pet but solely for the immediate area surrounding pet.

For those that tend to lack buying judgement the correct answer is (d)

Perspective from the Non-Dog-Owning World: Olfactory Sensation

There are near 8 billion people in the world all with different viewpoints. This adds complexity, as instead of seeing the similarities we share, we often focus on what is different, which leads to disagreements and fights. Simply understanding other points of view and attempting to see something from a different perspective could help many of these problems. Real Reddit post:

ARE SOME PEOPLE MORE SENSITIVE TO THE SMELL OF DOG?

A lot of people seem to not notice the fact that dogs, even after a bath, absolutely reek. I'm a bit of an outlier here in that I don't mind the occasional friendly dog as long as I have no responsibility for it and don't have to be cornered by the smell, but I hate how the smell of the dog gets transferred to my hands if I touch it and my hands reek until I get the chance to wash them. Dog smell is one of my least favorite smells in the world. It sticks around even if the dog left the room hours ago.

Is this something that dog owners genuinely don't perceive?

Know Your Limitations. The charges of Adorables are known for their zest and zeal but self-awareness can also be helpful. It may be that your motley crew of pups just should not accompany you when seeing friends for a visit or be at your side when you're out for dinner. Know your limitations and the limitations of others. If your crew is a rambunctious bunch and you were invited to a city apartment it may not be a fit regardless of your optimistic nature and your desires.

Knowing your Adorable's limitations also means knowing your limita-

A TRUE CAUTIONARY TAIL: KNOWING YOUR CHARGE: THE HABITUAL THIEF

Great Danes are obviously well known for their kitchen counter height. With that knowledge comes a need for their charges to be on high alert for items that could be licked, eaten, or drooled on that are inaccessible to other dogs.

There was once a Great Dane, Alice, as famous for her personality and adorableness as any Great Dane is, who always shadowed her charge, unless she was catching some Zs or thoughtfully taking stock of any food within reach. Due to her sheer adorableness and impenetrable bond with her charge she was typically included as a plus one. However, if her charge ever let her guard down the result would be take out for dinner, as opposed to the deliciously cooked meal prepared with

tions. If you prefer to pay attention to wine and chatter more than enforcing your host's rules regarding your Adorable you may want to leave him with some loving friends while you're out. Some rules require oversight and enforcement, for instance not eating from the counter. If you prefer to gossip with friends and know that your Great Dane can no more avoid that stick of butter on the table than you can decline a refreshing glass of bubbly in the afternoon then it's likely you will not be the best to keep a keen eye out and gently slide temptations out of reach, the results of which can be a disaster and create foes.

Use Your Inside Voice. Hosts appreciate guests, and guests get invited back, who are respectful of others. If in private they speak loudly with and at their Adorable, when in a group setting it is helpful to tone it down. Incessant chatter with your Adorable about the quality of his sleep or walk and a clicker training refresher at 6 a.m. may disrupt your host's slumber and cause more frustration than stepping in gum. Also, if another person yells loudly about how wonderful your Adorable is, you will be blamed. Each loud incursion is a check mark against you. More than three checks probably means you ain't comin' back.

Manage Waste. Pet waste management holds a great opportunity to demonstrate respectfulness to your host. The best way to approach this matter is to attempt to have your host not even be aware that your Adorable makes waste, both during your stay and after (no landmines to be discovered post departure). Discretely discover where the outdoor trash can is for your poop bags. Don't dispose of waste bags indoors and then be forced to manage discussions regarding the cause of a wretched smell. Indoor disposal is a signal to the host that deep down you really don't like them. Which is okay if they think that, it's just when you take a shower they will steal money out of your wallet.

Manners. Clarence Thomas guides us in this area with the credo, "Good manners will open doors that the best education will not." This, of course, doesn't apply

love, ensuring the plus one status did not occur twice at the same venue.

This included the time Alice was on the invite to a multiday adventure at a friend's remote mountain cabin. Alice and her charge were tasked with bringing a detailed and itemized grocery list consisting of difficult-to-procure organic, GF, keto items while the rest of the group trailered the horses. One item, which caused a significant delay and several grocery store stops in various remote towns, was organic butter. Finally, the most cherished butter was procured and dutifully kept safe until their arrival at the cabin.

Soon after their welcome and proud reveal of the prized butter, the organic, keto, GF, sustainable, and free-range produce, the items were set out on a picnic table. As soon as attention turned to cocktails, Alice saw her chance and quickly removed the organic butter. It vanished with only a few smacks of her lips as evidence of the deliciousness she'd experienced.

There was not a replacement for several hundred miles and to this day, many years after her passing she is remembered for the butter incident as opposed to her other incredible qualities, like sitting on the couch, turning on the TV and watching it, and her gentle way with puppies the size of her muzzle. Her charge knew her proclivity for butter and her help-herself attitude; she could, and should, have used that knowledge to ensure that the butter was in the cooler and Alice's pristine reputation could have been preserved along with sought-after piece of buttered toast.

No one knows if a large quantity of butter affects the arteries of Great Danes, but if it did, it was Alice's tastes and her charge's memory lapses that did Alice in. The World Dog Health Organization recommends that an Adorable only has one stick of butter in their lifetime for every 50 pounds of weight. Alice would have needed to weigh 2,500 pounds for that math to have contributed to her demise.

to doctors, lawyers, politicians, comedians, television executives, writers, farmers, or most careers. But it does apply to your Adorable where manners open doors to fans' hearts. Manners generally mean not chasing the cat, jumping on the sofa uninvited, caught with all fours standing on the dinner table, jumping on people with muddy paws, and being able to sit and come. Lapses in these areas may be forgiven relative to how cute your Adorable is.

Perspective from the Non-Dog-Owning World: Manners

As Adorable owners it may be hard to see the perspective of a non-dog host. This real Reddit post gets right to the heart of potential frustrations such people may face.

BREAKDOWN OF WHAT HAPPENED WHEN MY FRIEND BROUGHT OVER HIS "WELL-BEHAVED" DOGS

I have hiking trails within walking distance of my house and go hiking with my friend once every week or two. Last week I asked him if he wanted to come over and have a drink before we set out. He brought his two mid-sized dogs to hang out with us in the backyard. Here's what happened:

We have raised garden areas where we grow vegetables. My wife and I work on these every single day, so I asked my friend to make sure the dogs leave them alone. Naturally, one dog immediately runs and jumps into one of them at full speed.

Meanwhile the other one is pissing on our flowers.

My friend calls the dog out of our garden. It runs over and knocks over his drink.

It then goes over to my wife's drink and sticks its filthy tongue in it.

The other one is now taking a dump on our grass.

The first then jumps on my four-year-old son. He was scared but handled it well.

The one that was in my garden then started digging a hole in my shrubs border.

Same dog jumped in our garden AGAIN and trampled our bok choy.

Next thing we know one of the dogs is GONE. The backyard has a fence, but a dog can easily squeeze under. We spend the next 15 minutes searching the neighborhood for the damn dog.

There was more, but I'll stop here.

This was all over the course of 20 or 25 minutes. Absolute chaos. These dogs demanded constant attention from all three adults and completely ruined what should have been a pleasant time.

I can only imagine the damage they would do to the inside of a house.

In other Reddit threads, the same exact scenario takes place, but replace the word dog with four-year-olds, frat members, or home remodelers. (It's fun to read with the replaced names.)

Bring a gift. Show up wielding a gift to set the vibe of appreciation and thoughtfulness (with the graciousness attributed to your Adorable, of course). Typically, a hostess gift is something a host or hostess would use in the course of entertaining, however, our preference is to shower the hostess with an indulgent gift that acknowledges their efforts to make your time memorable. They are also the very person that passes ultimate judgment and are responsible for future invitations and therefore deserve something individual and special that

@pawsitivleypawsome FOLLOW ...

"No one has become poor by giving." -Anne Frank. Favorite products in our gift for our lovely hostess! #madrigalcreatives

may have a direct impact on such judgement. A gift basket of restorative wellness like those from madrigalcreatives.com will ultimately show you are thoughtful in your gifting, since everyone knows that the hostess does the mostest and deserves an indulgent treat for all the extra effort. During your visit you can see whether the basket was any good prior to buying one for someone else.

Say Thank You. A special note of thanks not only shows appreciation for the fun times but can ensure that your hostess has your digits for her Christmas card list and her future invites. A thank you card with a pic of your Adorable looking adorable will provide a lasting memory of him at his best and a paw signature will leave a happy imprint in their mind. If a small issue did arise during your stay do not bring it up but instead use the thank you note to relive a fond memory of your time together. If you have extra cards stuff them into windshield wipers at the airport.

Sample thank you note. Avoids mention of Harry's garbage issue, unwillingness to remove himself from the sofa so others could sit down, and his incessant begging at the dinner table. Instead highlights a positive experience and a desire to return:

Dear Jane and Mark,

Thank you so much for spending time with Harry and I this past weekend. Your home is incredible and hiking the hills with such stunning views will be remembered fondly. Harry proved his worth in chasing the coyotes away and has expressed that he hopes his stoic behavior will garner an invite for subsequent celebrations. We truly appreciate your hospitality and hope to see you soon.

With love and thanks,

Sarah and Harry

xoxo

A TRUE CAUTION-ARY TAIL: DOGS AND PLANES.

A story goes that a slight and energetic German shorthair, Shelby, set out on a quick trip from Seattle to San Francisco. She was provided with relaxants, placed in a not-so-spacious crate, and bid farewell as staff shuffled the crate towards the plane. On arrival in San Francisco her charge could not find her on the oversize luggage rack, nor on the luggage carousel, nor waiting with a suited airline worker. She was nowhere to be seen and after a brief discussion with those in charge, who are used to hearing hundreds of stories a day about lost black rollers, it was clear that Shelby was in the ether. The demeanor of customer service handling the report of a lost pet did not deviate from the demeanor applied when investigating a black roller filled with cardigans. As Shelby was described to the counter clerks, "Ugh, brown, medium-size, ALIVE," they reviewed their screen and declared

TRAVEL BASICS: GETTING TO AND FRO

Air Travel. This is a mode of transportation where you gain convenience but proportionately take on risk.

Risk that Harry does not appreciate his stowage under the seat on the plane and makes his displeasure known to the rest of the passengers.

Risk that something is ejected from Harry with a strong odor with five hours left on the flight.

Risk that any Adorable that is checked does not return, is shipped a thousand miles away, and has to make a trek back home that will take months. This could be turned into a movie but the airlines have lost so many Adorables that the studios are no longer interested in this storyline.

CALM COCKTAIL

A Calm cocktail may be your travel partner savior. Lines of people and pets, hands in face, prolonged time in a small crate, and the buzz and energy of travel may cause you and your Adorable to need to chill. A Calm cocktail has provided such support for many intrepid travelers to date. There is some question as to what makes the best Calm cocktail. Are pharmaceuticals superior to plant power? Is hemp the best? Is it important to arrive without brain fog or side effects or will you have to factor in a lazy day to overcome your Calm cocktail? Easy application and a fast-acting elixir are crucial, as an Adorable may need relief from travel anxiety fast. Treats containing relaxants are nice, but slower to work through the system and it may not be the time to ingest food, whereas a hemp tincture is a pain as it requires aim and is slow-working. For those that need an effective solution, spray four to five squirts of yummy chicken-flavored Calm, from Madrigal Pet Wellness, directly into your Adorable's mouth and see the calming effects in about 15-20 minutes. It goes without saying that you should consult your vet before administering anything or pretending that you are one.

that she was, "Gone."

Speculation and inquiry ensued: Was she on the tarmac, run over by a plane, in the airport bathroom, on her way to Egypt? Even as the investigation continued these questions could not be answered. Shelby was moving to a remote ranch in California due to her incredible energy and was being kicked out of Alaska for consistently escaping and streaking through the reindeer research station. This meant that, 1) Shelby's new home was far from the city airport, and 2) Shelby's amazing energy levels would prevent her from enjoying the confines of a dog crate.

After a nail-biting day, the airline found her. Roy, Shelby's driver, pulled up at a remote ranch in the Napa foothills at 2 a.m., Shelby, head out the window of the giant '72 convertible Cadillac. Roy announced, "I have Shelby here for ya. We had a fine time. She's a real good pup, and just finished a sandwich."

Airplane trips may not always end with a Roy and happy Shelby driving up at the end of them.

Be the Best Seatmate on the Plane

Just because your Adorable is under your seat or in the cargo hold and will be unable to serve as your confidante for the trip it does not mean that your neighbor is obligated to serve as your stand in. Be judicious about verbally throwing up on them; if there is an issue during your five plus hours together you want a gracious being in your vicinity as opposed to a worn-out, tense seatmate that is fed up with you. That negative energy can affect your Adorable, even at a distance.

CONVERSATION TOPICS TO AVOID WITH YOUR SEATMATE

- How smart your pet is. Additionally, a long diatribe detailing the multiple instances in which his intellect was revealed is a big no-no. It is amazing that your Adorable can fetch, swim in the ocean, and paddle board but if your seatmate is interested give him your IG handle and let him see for himself.

- How difficult it is on you to travel with your Adorable. It breaks your heart to have him in his carrier, he should be out entertaining us all, and wouldn't he like to meet Harry? Can your seatmate provide some cover from the attendants so he can come out and play?

- Itemized plans in your destination city with a play-by-play of your arrangements.

Detailed description of Harry's wellness routine and his diet. (Actually, anything detailed about anything.)

Danger zone: lifting one of your seatmate's headphones off his ear to tell him any of the above is particularly risky.

Dear Kendra,

I am a traveler who does not travel lightly. With the adoption of my Adorable, my travel staples have gotten even heavier making travel seem overwhelming! Jean-Pierre, my papillon and I, are scheduled to travel to France to embark on heritage tourism to learn more about Jean-Pierre's ancestry. Since our travelling will take us to the places, artifacts, and activities that authentically represent the stories of papillons of the past and present, by journeying to a place of their cultural identity we will be very busy and with too much baggage we may hold up the tour.

Can you help us travel a bit lighter? Here is my list of Jean-Pierre's items:

- Seven jackets with seven collar combinations

- Dog bed

- Mandatory crate for air travel

- Raw pet food and treats, and cooler to maintain temperature

- Special luvy blanket

- Large furry blanket to spread on furniture

- Special nightlight and sound machine with calming sleep noises for Jean-Pierre

- Supplement repertoire like super greens, oil of oregano, and elderberry to stop pathogens and keep immune system strong

- Compression socks to keep circulation while stuck in crate (even though will sneak out of crate throughout flight)

- Herbal essential oil towelettes

- Blue light glasses

- Poop scooper, baggies, and gloves

- Foldable fire hydrant

- Fake grass mat
- Red light for adjusting circadian rhythm and general health on arrival
- Sleep mask
- Case of toys, bones, and teeth cleaning devices
- First aid kit
- Calm and Relieve plus hemp sprays from Madrigal Pet Wellness

Thank you for any thoughts you may have to help us.

Kindly,
Cultural Travelers

....

Dear Cultural Travelers!

What an amazing trip you will have, especially since the papillon was from the Renaissance period. A cultural trip that includes experiences from such an era is sure to be an exciting one!

Honesty, I think your list for Jean-Pierre is perfect. Smart having a color-combination jacket for every day of the week and including some of the latest trends in biohacking such as the hemp sprays and blue blocking glasses, both essential for good sleep.

I suggest you take a long hard look at your own packing list and cut out nonessentials like too many shoes, which are notorious stowage hogs, and hair implements. No need for a curling iron, just pack a compact hat. Jean-Pierre's list looks great and is a reflection of a very well prepared Adorable.

Enjoy and travel safe and comfortable.

—Kendra

BREED SPOTLIGHT

Papillon. The little papillon was established during the Renaissance period in France as a companion dog for noble ladies. Papillons aren't simply lapdogs. These happy, playful little dogs have lots of energy. They can be rather spunky, a little needy, and expressive and are also known as vocal or incessant barkers.

THE ROAD TRIP

A few hours before you leave for your destination, start packing your vehicle. Procure the essentials from within the house and deposit in the vehicle in an orderly fashion. Dog beds should be placed in first so that their space is reserved, while the other necessities are organized around the dog bed, including water and luggage. After a few rounds of removing everything and reloading again in an attempt to optimize space to fit in that extra fluffy dog bed, the car is finally packed. You share a high five with your Adorable and then utter the words "Load up." You finally hit the open road and as you do Harry alternates comfortable snoozes in the back and enjoying the wind in his fur.

You will have forgotten something. Don't worry about it. You'll buy another one when you get there. It's very likely that when you pulled everything out of the car you forgot that you had set your wallet on the cooler and it is now in your driveway. So, you'd better turn back. If you are farther than 15 minutes away, just cancel all your cards on the phone at a rest stop as the neighborhood hooligans are already at Home Depot buying saws and hammers and rely on Apple Pay.

This is the story of an experienced Adorable. He has been on numerous short trips and, with time, increased the distance covered and the time spent in the car. He also has a dedicated area, spacious enough to stand, sit, turn around, or sleep in. The driver, and his charge, drive away with confidence knowing where they are going to stop to stretch their legs. These are the makings of a great road trip.

QUIZ

THE BIG TRAVEL QUIZ

Travelling itself is the big test but prior to departure take this test to see if you are ready to get your Adorable out in the world.

1 **What city consistently appears in the blogs of "Top Dog Cities in America?"**

A. Seattle

B. Miami

C. New Orleans

a. is the correct answer. Seattle is full of dog-friendly restaurants and cafés and is on a par with Paris. Miamians have not grasped the dog thing and in New Orleans, dogs are typically only found playing an instrument in the street for coins.

2 **How do you know if a hotel is dog friendly?**

A. Your credit card is charged a large pet deposit when you check in.

B. A sign at the front door indicates Service Dogs Only.

C. Doggie snacks are available at the front desk in a well-curated pet pack.

c. is the correct answer. Any hotel that goes to that effort needs to be tagged in your feed as a show of your appreciation. Just be sure that the picture posted does not make them regret their hospitable nature and include Harry drooling on the pillows.

3 **What city consistently appears in the blogs of "Top Dog Cities in America?"**

A. You buy a vest online that says "Service Dog" and he wears it.

B. Your dog is your confidante and during quarantine you could swear he answered back a few times.

C. Your vet has provided you with a certificate.

c. is correct. No one will argue that (a) and (b) should qualify but the law says (c) is it.

4 **You need to pick up your dog's waste when:**

A. There is a sign that says you need to.

B. Your pet goes on the grass or in the dog park when others are watching.

C. Anytime he goes.

c. is the correct answer, although we too wish (a) and (b) were true.

5 **You are considering a long road trip and wondering what works best with your Adorable's desires for modes of travel.**

A. Your Adorable loves to hang out between your neck and the seat rest.

B. Your Adorable is safely in the back snoozing on a dog bed or is restrained.

C. Your Adorable is really not keen on staying inside of a stuffy vehicle and elects to ride in the back of the truck with the wind in his face.

b. is the correct answer. There are freakish statistics about the speed at which an Adorable will move through the windshield in the event of a crash. If (a) was selected that would also include parts of you and (b) is incorrect since riding in a bed of a truck anytime other than a short trip to Walgreens or around the ranch is a bit much and your Adorable's lips may be left permanently splayed open.

If you got at least four correct you are ready for adventure!

CHAPTER 20

INSTA-ADORABLE:
KEEPING UP WITH YOUR PUP'S INSTAFAME

Although life as an Adorable is fun it is no longer the same as it once was. You have dutifully made it to the world of the Instafamous. You're somebody now.

Sure, you will miss the trips to the park without constant photo op interruptions, and enjoying holidays without the corresponding themed outfits (like the one with hearts where, for some reason, a tray of chocolates is left out for you to eat and then you're yelled at). But you have come this far in your journey and you were born to be Adorable so life was somewhat decided for you.

Being a celeb is a drain: you experience a renewed focus on your behavior, nutrition, and grooming. You hear the word "influencer" bandied around and you also seem to be out and about more, going to new venues and traveling in the car where no one cares if your head is out of the window, just as

Pre-Instafamous Memories

This Is ME

I'll Always Remember
THE TIME I ALMOST CAUGHT A SQUIRREL.

My favorite Activity
CHASING ALL SPECIES OF SQUIRRELS

This Year I learned . . .
TO STAY PUT IN MY POSE WHEN SOMETHING IS BEING POINTED AT ME AND A SQUIRREL IS NEARBY.

My Proudest Moment
REALIZING THAT IF I COULD CLIMB TREES OR FIT IN SQUIRREL HOLES I WOULD HAVE CAUGHT A SQUIRREL.

long as you don't lose the sunglasses. It seems that the camera is always pointed at you and now you finally remember where to look when they say the funny line, "Say 'fleas!'"

This is the good life, but there are times when you dream of the old days. Then just at that moment someone brings you a bacon-flavored treat on a tray and calls you sir or madam and you think, "Screw the old days. Go get me one of those small sausages and move your butt."

Influencer: Anyone who's built themselves an online reputation by doing and sharing awesome things online. To their audiences, influencers are tastemakers, trendsetters, and trusted experts whose opinions about certain subjects are respected. It's about money and a love for followers, but mostly money.

What the Adorable is noting above is that life has changed in subtle and unexpected ways. Once you embraced the influencer lifestyle, sponsorships began to appear along with podcast interviews, charity balls, and meetings with important people, which of course, continued to fuel your Insta fame. Your life is passing in front of your eyes. Before you know it, you are living in a different world.

STAGES of INSTAFAME

We just learned about these treats. Harry loves them! #sponsoredcontent

Checking out the sights, Paris, baby! #instagood

10,000-100,000 Followers

- Seek virtual assistant to manage the many product feature requests
- Develop media kit to distribute for influencer opportunities
- Consider feed in terms of original content and sponsored content
- Create business plan for own ecommerce business (to subsidize necessary photographer)
- Personal mishaps affect account growth
- Preoccupied with IG statistics like engagement rate

100,000+ Followers

- Virtual assistant manages influencer requests and event calendar
- New set of very famous friends that regularly appear in posts
- Engaged PR firm
- Necessity for original content and posting schedule requires international travel, charity events, and brand launches
- Just finished launch of second Harry branded product
- Personal mishaps require jail time
- Taking down celebs is the law of the jungle

CHAPTER 21

SPEAK! TERMINOLOGY AND LINGO TO BREAK INTO THE DOGGO BIG LEAGUES

Pet lovers and their Adorables have their own words and behaviors (used in lieu of words, in the case of dogs) but they also communicate certain facts that the English language simply cannot do properly. They create an instant connection and understanding with fellow pet lovers and with dogs themselves.

LEXICON

Those who share their lives with Adorables connect with others through their mutual love of Adorables and their appreciation for dogs' physical manifestations of adorableness. For the benefit of that camaraderie, they have developed a mode of communication, a codified set of terms, which have become popular hashtags and which create an even greater and instant sense of community.

FORMS OF

Over centuries, verbal and developed to enable between POWs, tapping on using sign language to adhering to their vows of silence.

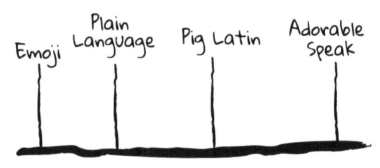

Emoji — Plain Language — Pig Latin — Adorable Speak

General public's increasing difficulty (from left to right)

COMMUNICATION

non-verbal language have communication, such as their cell walls, or monks communicate while still

to comprehend language

*Note: this is accurate at the time of writing but it is expected that Adorable Speak will be akin to plain language due to the proliferation of Adorables after publication of this book.

The community is based on a common affection towards dogs that ensures the "we hate dogs" Reddit subgroup cannot decode the conversation or will ever have cause to stumble on a clever hashtag and penetrate the community with their negativity and ignorance of the greatness of dogs.

DECODING HASHTAGS

Beans *n*. Adorably poofy paw pads. Hashtags and Posts: #toebeans 350,000 posts alone on Instagram as of this writing. There are some variations that include emojis, days of the week and such like #toebeantuesday, each of which is replete with creative pictures of pet toes. Warning: in some ancient cultures pet toes are considered valuable in warding off giants. So, some posts may not make total sense.

Boop *v*. A soft, sweet, loving tap on the nose. Hashtag #boopmynose 1.4m posts, #boop 1.1m, #boopboop 41.2m #boopthesnoot 269,000. How, you think, can there be so many nose shots? They really are mostly headshots. This should not be confused with #poopmynose which has 1b followers and regular appearances on every show that ends with "Funniest Home Videos."

Absolute Unit *n*. Not Brad Pitt but a huge, adorable giant; a majestic, exceptional hunk of a pet; the biggest, fluffiest, most large-and-in-charge pet you've ever seen. No particular hashtag use with this phrase but we foresee that changing. This has nothing to do with a 1970s adult film star by the same name.

Doggo *n*. Nicknames for when a pet is too cute to be called a mere dog or cat—similar to adding "*-ito*" on the end of a Spanish noun. No hashtag use but plenty of account use reflects the acceptance and embracing of this term like @doggosbeingdoggos with 509,000 followers and deliciously cute dog pictures. Strangely, 53 percent of men in Australia go by the nickname Doggo.

Mlem *n.* Pet's tongue sticking out. The length the tongue required to protrude to be considered a mlem may depend on your background. As of now there is not really a hashtag use but again, the large use of mlem in accounts is proof that the lexicon is accepted and recognized such as in accounts like @mlem.gram with a feed of all things pets and tongues, but to really capture the mlems #tongueouttuesday or #tots is your hashtag. The word mlem has only been typed and has never been spoken, except inadvertently by a person with a cold trying to explain that they have a lot of phlegm.

Sploot *n.* A split for the whole body, when a quadruped's belly is flat on the ground and their back legs are pointing straight out behind them. Accounts like @dogsploots are dedicated to the sploot. Ancient cave paintings have shown early dogs captured in frozen sploot poses, although some experts believe it was a running and jumping depiction, which is just crazy.

Blep *n.* A pet's tongue sticking out. To some, the word can be used interchangeably with mlem. Accounts like @whattheblep reflect this lexicon but to really get the hang of a tongue shot and a blep, @totuesday has it all. The word blep has only been typed and has never been spoken, except inadvertently by a person with a cold trying to explain that they need some assistance.

Derpy *adj.* Not confined to pets. Means clumsy, clueless, or silly-looking cats and dogs. The @derpy_huskies bio describes adventures of two derpy pups in the PNW, revealing that social media is proof of our ever-expanding lexicon. For years, the word derpy not only meant clumsy, but was also used to describe a pool of blood at the bottom of a staircase. This definition seems to have died out.

Bork *n.* A cuter substitute for bark. Doggos in particular will bork. As of this writing #bork has over 350,000 posts. Sometimes your dog will bork uncontrollably and sometimes he will fort uncontrollably.

Floof *n.* A pet with fluffy, cloudlike fur; the fur of an exceptionally fluffy pet. Floof can be used to describe both a very furry animal as well as their fur itself. Accounts like @floofcloudnine are excellent examples of the floof. Until it was banned in the 1950s floof blankets and carpeting were all the rage.

Floofy *adj.* A pet so fluffy that you absolutely need to pet them immediately. You can see this adjective illustrated very well in accounts like @floofy. winnie. Walt Disney's first ever cartoon character before Mickey Mouse was Floofy Dog, until it was banned in the 1950s.

Smol *n.* Tiny and adorable and unbearably cute pets. @smol.posts with 190k followers and no original content shows the recognition of this lexicon in use. It is now clear that bad spellers and annunciators rule the world.

Adorable adj.

The origins of the word adorable are religious; it was first used only to mean "worthy of adoration." The Latin word *adorare*, "to ask in prayer," is the root of adore, which in the 14th century meant "to worship." It wasn't until the 1880s that adorable began to mean "delightful" rather than "worthy of worshiping."

The adorable video quickly went viral with tens of thousands of shares and comments within a few days.

Fox News, October 8, 2020

*Vocabulary.com

BETWEEN DOGS: MAY BE OVERHEARD AT THE DOG PARK

Dogs love to talk. Along with the 46 different types of bark noted by scientists to emanate from a sheep dog, they also communicate amongst themselves in other forms of dog speak. Here is some that you may overhear:

DOG SPEAK HEARD AT THE PARK

Play Bow

Let's play

Paw Slap

Hey Buddy

Rearing Up on Hind Legs
(Sign of affection)

Eight Ways to Refer to an Adorable

Canine	Pal*
Puppy	Tyke**
Pooch	Furry Friend***
Dude*	Dawg****
Bud*	

*Interchangeable with your two-legged pals

**Interchangeable with a young toddler in the family or outside of it

***Interchangeable with a feline but not certain hairless breeds

**** Likely better used to refer only to a cheating boyfriend. Usually preceded by the phrase, "You rotten, miserable, cheatin', bastard…"

PAWSOME PUNS

Referred to both as the lowest form of humor and a powerful tool to convey complex ideas, puns are oft used lexicon in the land of Adorables.

Some say they allow the user to pack more meaning, or more layers of meaning, into fewer words, which is often necessary. For whatever reason, puns are revered by the charges of Adorables and why not?

Puns are used in every language and even at the signing of the Declaration of Independence, where Benjamin Franklin is famously quoted as saying, "We must all hang together or assuredly we shall all hang separately." Then George Washington famously told Ben, "You will deny me three times before the cock crows thrice." To which Ben replied, "George just said thrice."

There is no logical reason why puns and pups go together especially well but maybe it's the need to relay those complex ideas. You may hear the following puns in conversation. Here is a snapshot so you won't be concerned and look quizzically at the deliverer of a pun while your mind doubles back in confusion and you miss the point entirely.

- Do you want us to groom you, cutie? Fur sure!

- How's Harry doing today? He's pawsome!

- Is it FriYAY yet? It's been a ruff week.

- I'm glad you made it! Yes, we made it to the pawty!

- Paws for the holidays.

- (At a family dinner.) We're thankful for our friends and fur our puppy.

- I love you furry much!

- Did your dog do that? It's paw-ssible!

- You're pawtastic!

- I can't find my dog. Okay, let's spread out and stay pawsitive!

- Barking it from the wooftops!

- The pup emBARKed on a new journey.

- So, I see Harry's been acting up. Yes, that's why we're getting a new LEASH on life!

- Bone-appétit!

- Your dog loves you so much. Yes, we have the ulti-mutt friendship.

DEVICES TO FOSTER COMMUNICATION WITH YOUR ADORABLE

Technology is developing at an overwhelming speed. But what remains unclear is how fast we are advancing as a result, especially as it relates to our canine relationships.

Moore's law was the first to shine a light on the technology growth rate. It says that the transistor count on integrated circuits doubles roughly every two years. But technology seems to finally be reaching its limits of usefulness and the growth rate appears to proportionately be revealing a similar decline in our judgement, making the strict interpretation of Moore's law less plausible.

Take these inventions birthed to improve the communications with our Adorables:

BarkingMat. The sellers' of the BarkingMat let you know that you can place the BarkingMat by the door and as soon as your dog steps on it, you'll receive a notification. Your dog will literally be texting you from the other room letting you know when he needs to take care of business. Be forewarned the advertising shows multiple puppies playing and jumping on the matt which could lead some to block the serial texter thereby defeating the purpose, no worries, the mat can withstand accidents.

PetChatz. Described as a luxury Greet and Treat two-way videophone that provides a full day of interaction and entertainment for your home alone pet. According to PetChatz creators features include: two-way audio-visual interaction, Sound & motion triggered smart video recording, pet camera feature, and treat dispersal. You can actually dispense treats to your pet four different ways without even being in the same room as him! Your dog can call you on the pet camera feature and message you and play games with the PawCall accessory. There is even an aromatherapy feature (for the dog) which diffuses calming aromatherapy to ease anxiety while he streams DOGTV or wonders why he cannot just see you in person.

TOP ALTERNATIVE COMMUNICATION DEVICES
(TO COMMUNICATE WITH AND BY YOUR ADORABLE)

In addition to, yelling, talking, facial expressions and gestures, these are top tools that are used to interact with your Adorable

- Clicker

- Blow horn

- Whoopee cushion

- Bell on doorknob (or anywhere)

- Car horn

- Electric collar

- Telephone

- Augmentative and Alternative Communication (AAC) Devices[8]

- Alexa

This is the end of the book but only the beginning of your flourishing life with your Adorable. By now your Adorable is known by some, found irresistible by all, and living a fulfilled life with you happily at his side. You have chosen a path, fit in your groove, settled in a home, created a stellar online presence, and are maybe thinking of adding a roommate. You are enjoying every one of life's milestones with your Adorable.

This is not the end—go forth and enjoy many more milestones. It is your right and the right of others to meet your bestie, virtually at least!

---

8   ***How Stella Learned to Talk*** by Christina Hunger chronicles the journey that Christina and Stella have taken together, from the day they met, to the day Stella "spoke" her first word, and reveals the techniques Christina used to teach Stella, over thirty words with an ACC device.

ACKNOWLEDGEMENT

I am profoundly appreciative of my little grey pony Sinbad who from the age of five frequently dumped me in the mud or on the sand and caused plenty of heartache and certain joy but also without the resilience and tenacity he taught me there would be no book and surely not as many adventures to learn from to put in a book. My mom who was always there when I landed in the mud with the statement "you have to fall off 1000 times to be a good rider" which forged the connection between having the tenacity to get back on all while knowing there were 999 more times to fall and a life well-loved.

Of course, there would be no experiences to put in this book without all my furry dog pals that have been with me during every dump of Sinbad (likely caused many of them) and every milestone and will be with me forever more as life is just better with an Adorable (and a horse).

With gratitude I acknowledge my family for cherishing my children so much that their lives are better for it and especially my husband for loving dogs and from our first meeting accepting my Great Dane Alice as his own which has become a metaphor for our life.

Thank you to my children for your patience and love and learning that one more minute is not really that and loving dogs almost as much as I do.

Lightning Source UK Ltd.
Milton Keynes UK
UKHW021947101121
393761UK00007B/139